Cambridge Practice Tests for IELTS 1

MEDICAL LIBRARY

Vanessa Jakeman
Clare McDowell

CAMBRIDGE
UNIVERSITY PRESS

PUBLISHED BY THE PRESS SYNDICATE OF THE UNIVERSITY OF CAMBRIDGE
The Pitt Building, Trumpington Street, Cambridge CB2 1RP, United Kingdom

CAMBRIDGE UNIVERSITY PRESS
The Edinburgh Building, Cambridge CB2 2RU, UK
40 West 20th Street, New York, NY 10011–4211, USA
477 Williamstown Road, Port Melbourne, VIC 3207, Australia
Ruiz de Alarcón 13, 28014 Madrid, Spain
Dock House, The Waterfront, Cape Town, South Africa

http://www.cambridge.org

First published 1996
Tenth printing 2002

Printed in the United Kingdom at the University Press, Cambridge

ISBN 0 521 49767 1 Self-Study Student's Book
ISBN 0 521 49766 3 Set of 2 cassettes

Contents

Acknowledgements

We would like to thank the staff and students of the following institutions for their assistance in trialling these materials:
Wollongong English Language Centre; Australian College of English, Sydney; Hong Kong Polytechnic; Waratah Education Centre, Sydney; International House, Queensland; Milton English Language Centre, Sydney; Oxford Academy of English.
In addition, a number of our non-English speaking friends were kind enough to trial the materials in their early formats.

The authors and publishers are grateful to the following for permission to reproduce copyright material.
Focus magazine for the extract on pp. 20–21 from *A spark, a flint: how fire lept to life*; *BBC WILDLIFE Magazine* for the extract on pp. 24–5 from *Showboat as Ark*; *The Guardian* for the extract on pp. 28–9 from *Architecture – Reaching for the Sky* by Ruth Coleman and for the graphs on pp. 31 and 72; Geoff Maslen for the extract on pp. 40–41 from *The Rights of the Left*, published by *Good Weekend* magazine; *National Geographic* magazine for the extract and map on pp. 44–5 from *America's Beekeepers: Hives for Hire* by Alan Mairson, *National Geographic*, May 1993, and for the extract on pp. 80–81 from *Glass: Capturing the Dance of Light* by William S. Ellis, *National Geographic*, December 1993; the extract on pp. 48–9 is reprinted from *The Tourist Gaze*, © John Urry 1990, by permission of Sage Publications Ltd; *The European* for the extract on pp. 60–61 from *Spoken Corpus Comes to Life*, for the extract on pp. 64–5 from *Hobbits happy as homes go underground*, and for the extract on pp. 84–5 from *Why some women cross the finish line ahead of men* by Andrew Crisp; The Royal Zoological Society of New South Wales for the extract on pp. 87–8 from an article by Hugh Possingham in *Conservation of Australia's Forest Fauna*; Moulinex/Swan for the extract and illustrations on pp. 94–5 from *Instructions for a Moulinex Iron*; Cambridge Coach Services for the extract on p. 96; International Students House for the extracts on p. 99 and p. 101 from the *International Students' A–Z: A guide to studying and living in London*; Gore and Osment Publications for the diagram on p. 51 and the extract on pp. 102–3 from *The Science and Technology Project Book*; *BBC Good Food Magazine* for the extract from *Space Invaders*, *BBC Good Food Magazine*, January 1995, on which Practice Test 3, Listening, Section 4 is based; University of Westminster for the extract from *Getting it right: Essential information for international students* on which Practice Test 4, Listening, Section 2 is based; the IELTS Reading and Listening answer sheets are reproduced by permission of the University of Cambridge Local Examinations Syndicate.

Photographs: p. 20 The Science Photo Library/Adam Hart-Davis; p. 80 (top) Image Bank; p. 80 (bottom) Damien Lovegrove.

The illustration on p. 84 is reproduced by permission of Min Cooper/*The European*. The drawings are by Julian Page. Maps and diagrams by HardLines.

Book design by Peter Ducker MSTD

The cassette recording was produced by James Richardson at Studio AVP, London.

Introduction

TO THE STUDENT

About the book

This book has been written for candidates preparing for the revised version of the International English Language Testing System, known as IELTS. This is a test designed to assess the English language skills of non-English speaking students seeking to study in an English speaking country.

Aims of the book

- to prepare you for the test by familiarising you with the types of texts and tasks that you will meet in the IELTS test, and the level and style of language used in the test.
- to help you prepare for your studies at university or college by introducing you to the types of communication tasks which you are likely to meet in an English speaking study environment.

Content of the book

The book contains four complete sample IELTS tests, each comprising Listening and Speaking modules and Academic Reading and Writing modules. In addition there is one set of the General Training Reading and Writing modules. (NB all candidates do the same Listening and Speaking modules.) To accompany the tests there is an answer key at the back of the book and you should refer to this after you have attempted each of the practice tests. Also included is an annotated copy of the listening tapescripts with the appropriate sections highlighted to help you to check your answers. In addition, you will find one model answer for each type of writing task to guide you with your writing. There is a comprehensive key for the Reading and Listening sections, but if you are in any doubt about your answers, talk to a teacher or an English speaking friend. Where you are required to answer in your own words, the answer must be accurate in both meaning as well as grammar in order to be scored correct.

Benefits of studying for IELTS

By studying for IELTS you will not only be preparing for the test but also for your future as a student in an English speaking environment. The test is designed to assess your ability to understand and produce written and spoken language in an educational context. The book makes reference to the ways in which university study is organised in many English speaking countries and the types of academic tasks you will be expected to perform.

These include:
- Reading and understanding written academic or training language
- Writing assignments in an appropriate style for university study or within a training context
- Listening to and comprehending spoken language in both lecture format as well as formal and informal conversational style
- Speaking to colleagues and lecturers on general and given topics in formal and informal situations

Description of the test

There are two versions of the IELTS test:

Academic Module for students seeking entry to a university or institution of higher education offering degree and diploma courses	General Training Module for students seeking entry to a secondary school or to vocational training courses

Note: All candidates must take a test for each of the four skills: listening reading, writing and speaking. All candidates take the same Listening and Speaking modules but may choose between the Academic or General Training versions of the Reading and Writing sections of the test. You should seek advice from a teacher or a student adviser if you are in any doubt about whether to sit for the Academic modules or the General Training modules. **The two do not carry the same weight and are not interchangeable.**

Test format

<table>
<tr><td colspan="3" align="center">Listening
4 sections, around 40 questions
30 minutes + transfer time</td></tr>
<tr>
<td align="center">Academic Reading
3 sections, around 40 questions
60 minutes</td>
<td align="center">OR</td>
<td align="center">General Training Reading
3 sections, around 40 questions
60 minutes</td>
</tr>
<tr>
<td align="center">Academic Writing
2 tasks
60 minutes</td>
<td align="center">OR</td>
<td align="center">General Training Writing
2 tasks
60 minutes</td>
</tr>
<tr><td colspan="3" align="center">Speaking
10 to 15 minutes (11 to 14 minutes from July 2001)</td></tr>
<tr><td colspan="3" align="center">Total test time
2 hours 45 minutes</td></tr>
</table>

WHAT DOES THE TEST CONSIST OF?

The Listening Module

Requirements	Situation types	Question types
You must listen to four separate sections and answer questions as you listen. You will hear the tape *once only*. There will be between 38 and 42 questions. The test will take about 30 minutes. There will be time to read the questions during the test and time to transfer your answers on to the answer sheet at the end of the test. The level of difficulty of the texts and tasks increases through the paper.	The first two sections are based on social situations. There will be a conversation between two speakers and then a monologue. The second two sections are related to an educational or training context. There will be a conversation with up to four speakers and a lecture or talk of general academic interest.	You will meet a variety of question types which may include: • multiple choice • short answer questions • sentence completion • notes/summary/flow chart/table completion • labelling a diagram which has numbered parts • matching

Academic Reading Module

Requirements	Types of material	Question types
You must read three reading passages with a total of 1,500 to 2,500 words. There will be between 38 and 42 questions. You will have 60 minutes to answer all the questions. The level of difficulty of the texts and tasks increases through the paper.	Magazines, journals, textbooks and newspapers. Topics are not discipline specific but all are in a style appropriate and accessible to candidates entering postgraduate and undergraduate courses.	You will meet a variety of question types, which may include: • multiple choice • short answer questions • sentence completion • notes/summary/flow chart/table completion • choosing from a bank of headings • identification of writer's views or attitudes (Yes/No/Not given) • classification • matching lists • matching phrases

Academic Writing Module

Requirements	Task types
You must complete two writing tasks. You will have 60 minutes to complete both tasks.	*Task 1* You will have to look at a diagram, a table or short piece of text and then present the information in your own words.
You should spend about 20 minutes on Task 1 and write at least 150 words.	Your writing will be assessed on your ability to: • organise, present and compare data • describe the stages of a process • describe an object or event • explain how something works You will also be judged on your ability to: • answer the question without straying from the topic • write in a way which allows your reader to follow your ideas • use English grammar and syntax accurately • use appropriate language in terms of register, style and content
You should spend about 40 minutes on Task 2 and write at least 250 words.	*Task 2* You will have to present an argument or discuss a problem. Your writing will be assessed on your ability to: • present the solution to a problem • present and justify an opinion • compare and contrast evidence and opinions • evaluate and challenge ideas, evidence or an argument You will also be judged on your ability to: • communicate an idea to the reader in an appropriate style • address the problem without straying from the topic • use English grammar and syntax accurately • use appropriate language in terms of register, style and content

General Training Reading Module

Requirements	Types of material	Question types
You must answer questions on three sections of increasing difficulty with a total of 1,500 to 2,500 words. There will be between 38 and 42 questions. You will have 60 minutes to answer all the questions. The level of difficulty of the texts and tasks increases through the paper.	Notices, advertisements, booklets, newspapers, leaflets, timetables, books and magazine articles. *Section 1* Social survival – retrieving factual information *Section 2* Training survival – language in a training context *Section 3* General reading – extended prose with emphasis on descriptive and instructive texts of general interest	You will meet a variety of question types, which may include: • multiple choice • short answer questions • sentence completion • notes/summary/flow chart/table completion • choosing from a bank of headings • identification of writer's views or attitudes (Yes/No/ Not given) • classification • matching lists • matching phrases

General Training Writing Module

Requirements	Task types
You must complete two writing tasks. You will have 60 minutes to complete both tasks.	*Task 1* You will have to write a short letter in response to a given problem or situation. Your writing will be assessed on your ability to: • engage in personal correspondence • elicit and provide general factual information • express needs, wants, likes and dislikes • express opinions
You should spend about 20 minutes on Task 1 and write at least 150 words.	You will also be judged on your ability to: • answer the question without straying from the topic • write in a way which allows your reader to follow your ideas • use English grammar and syntax accurately • use appropriate language in terms of register, style and content
You should spend about 40 minutes on Task 2 and write at least 250 words.	*Task 2* You will have to present an argument or discuss a problem. Your writing will be assessed on your ability to: • provide general factual information • outline a problem and present a solution • present and justify an opinion You will also be judged on your ability to: • communicate an idea to the reader in an appropriate style • address the problem without straying from the topic • use English grammar and syntax accurately • use appropriate language in terms of register, style and content

The Speaking Module (A revised Speaking Module will be operational from July 2001. See page 155 for details.)

Requirements	Assessment criteria
You will have to talk to an examiner for about 15 minutes. The interview will be recorded. It is in 5 parts:	You will be assessed on the following criteria: • ability to communicate effectively • ability to use appropriate vocabulary and structures • ability to ask questions • ability to take initiative in a conversation • general fluency • structural accuracy • intelligibility
1 Introduction – Basic introductions	
2 Extended discourse – You will talk at some length about general topics of relevance or interest which will involve explanation and description.	
3 Elicitation – You will be given a cue card which describes a situation or problem. You must ask the examiner questions to obtain information.	
4 Speculation and attitudes – You will be asked to talk about your plans or proposed course of study. You should demonstrate your ability to speculate or defend a point of view.	
5 Conclusion – The interview comes to an end.	

How is IELTS scored?

IELTS provides a profile of your ability to use English. In other words your IELTS result will consist of a score in each of the four skills (listening, reading, writing, speaking) which is then averaged to give the Overall Band Score or final mark. Performance is rated in each skill on a scale of 9 to 1. The nine overall Bands and their descriptive statements are as follows:

9 Expert user

Has fully operational command of the language: appropriate, accurate and fluent with complete understanding.

8 Very good user

Has fully operational command of the language with only occasional unsystematic inaccuracies and inappropriacies. Misunderstandings may occur in unfamiliar situations. Handles complex detailed argumentation well.

7 Good user

Has operational command of the language, though with occasional inaccuracies, inappropriacies and misunderstandings in some situations. Generally handles complex language well and understands detailed reasoning.

6 Competent user

Has generally effective command of the language despite inaccuracies, inappropriacies and misunderstandings. Can use and understand fairly complex language, particularly in familiar situations.

5 Modest user

Has partial command of the language, coping with overall meaning in most situations, though is likely to make many mistakes. Should be able to handle basic communication in own field.

4 Limited user

Basic competence is limited to familiar situations. Has frequent problems in understanding and expression. Is not able to use complex language.

3 Extremely limited user

Conveys and understands only general meaning in very familiar situations. Frequent breakdowns in communication occur.

2 Intermittent user

No real communication is possible except for the most basic information using isolated words or short formulae in familiar situations and to meet immediate needs. Has great difficulty understanding spoken and written English.

1 Non user

Essentially has no ability to use the language beyond possibly a few isolated words.

0 Did not attempt the test

No assessable information provided.

What is the pass mark?

There is no fixed pass mark in IELTS. The institution you want to enter will decide whether your score is appropriate for the demands of the course of study or training you want to undertake. However, as a general rule, scores below Band 5 in any one skill are considered too low for academic study; scores above Band 6 are deemed to be adequate to good. Overall Band scores of 5 or 6 are borderline and may not be acceptable at many institutions. If you are getting only about half of the questions in these sample tests correct, then you are probably not quite ready to take the IELTS test. Again you should seek advice from a teacher about your level of English. Remember you must allow a duration of at least 3 months between each attempt at the test.

For further information about the test, see the IELTS Handbook available from all test centres and also from UCLES (University of Cambridge Local Examinations Syndicate), from IDP Education Australia and from British Council Centres.

HOW TO USE THIS BOOK

The tests in this book are similar in length, format and content to the real test, but success in these tests will not guarantee success in the real test. It often seems easier to work on practice materials than to sit the tests themselves because you are not under the same pressure.

Timing
In order to maximise your use of these tests, you should make a note of the time it takes you to answer each of the sections. As you progress through the book, be stricter with yourself about the time you allow yourself to complete the sections.

Answer sheets
When you sit for the real IELTS test, you will have answer sheets on which to write your answers. A sample of these is given at the end of this book. To help you prepare for the test, we suggest that you write your answers on separate sheets of paper, rather than in the book itself.

Answer keys
Listening
In addition to the answer key, you will find tapescripts for all of the listening passages. These have been annotated to show where in the text the answer to each question can be found. There is very often a signpost word which will cue your listening. Look out for these signposts. Remember, the answers are usually short and never more than three words. Read the questions carefully, in the time provided on the tape, before you listen to each section of the tape.

Reading

You will meet a number of different question types in the IELTS test. It is a useful strategy to become familiar with them and learn how best to approach them. The answer keys at the back of this book not only provide you with the answer to each question, but also give a suggested approach to each type of question, so take the time to work through them carefully.

Writing

You will find four sample answers to the writing tasks, one for each task type on each module. These have been included to give you an *idea* of the type of writing expected. However, there will be alternative approaches to each question and the model answers given should not be seen as prescriptive. Look carefully at the description of the writing test (given above in the Introduction) to see exactly which criteria you should be paying attention to in each task.

Speaking

The sample speaking tasks are to help you prepare for part 3 of the Speaking test. Remember that the examiner will expect you to show how much English you know and it is up to you to demonstrate that. You are expected to ask a lot of questions in part 3 and the examiner will not speak very much and may even appear to be 'unhelpful' at times, to encourage you to ask more questions. The sample speaking tasks include suggested examiner's prompts so that you can see how the interaction might unfold. It may be a useful preparation strategy to work with a friend and practise the interview format in this way, using the sample tasks in the book.

Note: A revised Speaking Module will be operational from July 2001. See page 155 for details and sample tasks.

Practice Tests

Practice Test 1

SECTION 1   *Questions 1–10*

Questions 1–5

Circle the appropriate letter.

> *Example*
> What has the woman lost?
>
> (A)   a briefcase   **C**   a handbag
> **B**   a suitcase   **D**   a wallet

1   What does her briefcase look like?

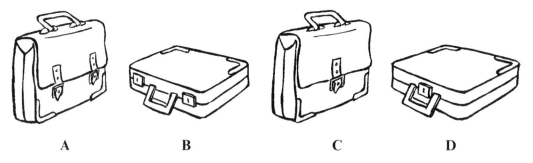

A   B   C   D

2   Which picture shows the distinguishing features?

A   B   C   D

3   What did she have inside her briefcase?

   A   wallet, pens and novel   **C**   pens and novel
   B   papers and wallet   **D**   papers, pens and novel

12

4   Where was she standing when she lost her briefcase?

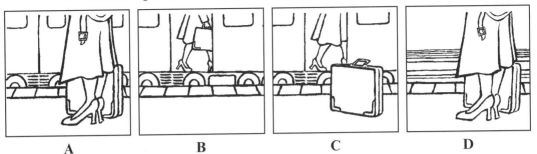

A   B   C   D

5   What time was it when she lost her briefcase?

A   B   C   D

Questions 6–10

Complete the form. Write NO MORE THAN THREE WORDS for each answer.

PERSONAL DETAILS FORM

Name: Mary **(6)** ....

Address: Flat 2

   (7) ....   **(8)** ....*Road*

   Canterbury

Telephone: (9) ....

Estimated value of lost item: (10) £ ....

SECTION 2   *Questions 11–21*

Questions 11–13

*Tick the **THREE** other items which are mentioned in the news headlines.*

NEWS HEADLINES	
A Rivers flood in the north	☐
Example **B** Money promised for drought victims	☑
C Nurses on strike in Melbourne	☐
D Passengers rescued from ship	☐
E Passengers rescued from plane	☐
F Bus and train drivers national strike threat	☐
G Teachers demand more pay	☐
H New uniform for QANTAS staff	☐
I National airports under new management	☐

Questions 14–21

Complete the notes below by writing **NO MORE THAN THREE WORDS** *in the spaces provided.*

The Government plans to give **(14)** $.. to assist the

farmers. This money was to be spent on improving Sydney's

(15) .... but has now been re-allocated.

Australia has experienced its worst drought in over fifty years.

Farmers say that the money will not help them because it is

(16) ....

An aeroplane which was carrying a group of **(17)** ....

was forced to land just **(18)** .... minutes after take-off.

The passengers were rescued by **(19)** .... The

operation was helped because of the good weather. The passengers

thanked the **(20)** .... for saving their lives but

unfortunately they lost their **(21)** ....

SECTION 3   *Questions 22–31*

Questions 22–31

Circle the appropriate letter.

Example
The student is looking for the School of
    A   Fine Arts.
    B   Economic History.
    Ⓒ   Economics.
    D   Accountancy.

---

22   The orientation meeting

    A   took place recently.
    B   took place last term.
    C   will take place tomorrow.
    D   will take place next week.

23   Attendance at lectures is

    A   optional after 4 pm.
    B   closely monitored.
    C   difficult to enforce.
    D   sometimes unnecessary.

24   Tutorials take place

    A   every morning.
    B   twice a week.
    C   three mornings a week.
    D   three afternoons a week.

25   The lecturer's name is

    A   Roberts.
    B   Rawson.
    C   Rogers.
    D   Robertson.

Questions 26–31

Complete the notes below using **NO MORE THAN THREE WORDS.**

Course requirements:

Tutorial paper:

A piece of work on a given topic. Students must:

- **(26)** .... *for 25 minutes*

- **(27)** ....

- *give to lecturer for marking*

Essay topic:

Usually **(28)** ....

Type of exam:

(29) ....

Library:

Important books are in **(30)** ....

Focus of course:

Focus on **(31)** ....

SECTION 4   *Questions 32–41*

Questions 32–33

Circle the appropriate letter.

32   The speaker works within the Faculty of

    A   Science and Technology.
    B   Arts and Social Sciences.
    C   Architecture.
    D   Law.

33   The Faculty consists firstly of

    A   subjects.
    B   degrees.
    C   divisions.
    D   departments.

Questions 34–36

Complete the notes in ***NO MORE THAN THREE WORDS****.*

The subjects taken in the first semester in this course are psychology, sociology,

(34) .... and

....

Students may have problems with

(35) .... and

(36) ....

Questions 37–41

Circle the appropriate letter.

37 The speaker says students can visit her

A   every morning.
B   some mornings.
C   mornings only.
D   Friday morning.

38 According to the speaker, a tutorial

A   is a type of lecture.
B   is less important than a lecture.
C   provides a chance to share views.
D   provides an alternative to groupwork.

39 When writing essays, the speaker advises the students to

A   research their work well.
B   name the books they have read.
C   share work with their friends.
D   avoid using other writers' ideas.

40 The speaker thinks that plagiarism is

A   a common problem.
B   an acceptable risk.
C   a minor concern.
D   a serious offence.

41 The speaker's aims are to

A   introduce students to university expectations.
B   introduce students to the members of staff.
C   warn students about the difficulties of studying.
D   guide students round the university.

READING

READING PASSAGE 1

*You should spend about 20 minutes on **Questions 1–15** which are based on Reading Passage 1 below.*

A spark, a flint: How fire leapt to life

The control of fire was the first and perhaps greatest of humanity's steps towards a life-enhancing technology

To early man, fire was a divine gift randomly delivered in the form of lightning, forest fire or burning lava. Unable to make flame for themselves, the earliest peoples probably stored fire by keeping slow-burning logs alight or by carrying charcoal in pots.

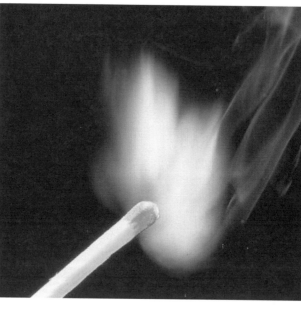

How and where man learnt how to produce flame at will is unknown. It was probably a secondary invention, accidentally made during tool-making operations with wood or stone. Studies of primitive societies suggest that the earliest method of making fire was through friction. European peasants would insert a wooden drill in a round hole and rotate it briskly between their palms. This process could be speeded up by wrapping a cord around the drill and pulling on each end.

The Ancient Greeks used lenses or concave mirrors to concentrate the sun's rays and burning glasses were also used by Mexican Aztecs and the Chinese.

Percussion methods of fire-lighting date back to Paleolithic times, when some Stone Age tool-makers discovered that chipping flints produced sparks. The technique became more efficient after the discovery of iron, about 5000 years ago. In Arctic North America, the Eskimos produced a slow-burning spark by striking quartz against iron pyrites, a compound that contains sulphur. The Chinese lit their fires by striking porcelain with bamboo. In Europe, the combination of steel, flint and tinder remained the main method of fire-lighting until the mid-19th century.

Fire-lighting was revolutionised by the discovery of phosphorus, isolated in 1669 by a German alchemist trying to transmute silver into gold. Impressed by the element's combustibility, several 17th century chemists used it to manufacture fire-lighting devices, but the results were dangerously inflammable. With phosphorus costing the equivalent of several hundred pounds per ounce, the first matches were expensive. .

The quest for a practical match really began after 1781 when a group of French chemists came up with the *Phosphoric Candle* or *Ethereal Match*, a sealed glass tube containing a twist of paper tipped with phosphorus. When the tube was broken, air rushed in, causing the phosphorus to self-combust. An even more hazardous device, popular in America, was the *Instantaneous Light Box* – a bottle filled with sulphuric acid into which splints treated with chemicals were dipped.

The first matches resembling those used today were made in 1827 by John Walker, an English pharmacist who borrowed the formula from a military rocket-maker called Congreve. Costing a shilling a box, *Congreves* were splints coated with sulphur and tipped with potassium chlorate. To light them, the user drew them quickly through folded glass paper.

Walker never patented his invention, and three years later it was copied by a Samuel Jones, who marketed his product as *Lucifers.* About the same time, a French chemistry student called Charles Sauria produced the first 'strike-anywhere' match by substituting white phosphorus for the potassium chlorate in the Walker formula. However, since white phosphorus is a deadly poison, from 1845 match-makers exposed to its fumes succumbed to necrosis, a disease that eats away jaw-bones. It wasn't until 1906 that the substance was eventually banned.

That was 62 years after a Swedish chemist called Pasch had discovered non-toxic red or amorphous phosphorus, a development exploited commercially by Pasch's compatriot J E Lundstrom in 1885. Lundstrom's safety matches were safe because the red phosphorus was non-toxic; it was painted on to the striking surface instead of the match tip, which contained potassium chlorate with a relatively high ignition temperature of 182 degrees centigrade.

America lagged behind Europe in match technology and safety standards. It wasn't until 1900 that the Diamond Match Company bought a French patent for safety matches – but the formula did not work properly in the different climatic conditions prevailing in America and it was another 11 years before scientists finally adapted the French patent for the US.

The Americans, however, can claim several 'firsts' in match technology and marketing. In 1892 the Diamond Match Company pioneered book matches. The innovation didn't catch on until after 1896, when a brewery had the novel idea of advertising its product in match books. Today book matches are the most widely used type in the US, with 90 percent handed out free by hotels, restaurants and others.

Other American innovations include an anti-afterglow solution to prevent the match from smouldering after it has been blown out; and the waterproof match, which lights after eight hours in water.

Questions 1–8

Complete the summary below. Choose your answers from the box at the bottom of the page and write them in boxes 1–8 on your answer sheet.

NB   *There are more words than spaces so you will not use them all.*
     You may use any of the words more than once.

EARLY FIRE-LIGHTING METHODS

> Primitive societies saw fire as a ... (*Example*) ... gift.   *Answer* heavenly

They tried to ... **(1)** ... burning logs or charcoal ... **(2)** ... that they could create fire themselves. It is suspected that the first man-made flames were produced by ... **(3)** ...

The very first fire-lighting methods involved the creation of ... **(4)** ... by, for example, rapidly ... **(5)** ... a wooden stick in a round hole. The use of ... **(6)** ... or persistent chipping was also widespread in Europe and among other peoples such as the Chinese and ... **(7)** ... . European practice of this method continued until the 1850s ... **(8)** ... the discovery of phosphorus some years earlier.

List of Words

Mexicans	random	rotating
despite	preserve	realising
sunlight	lacking	heavenly
percussion	chance	friction
unaware	without	make
heating	Eskimos	surprised
until	smoke	

Questions 9–15

Look at the following notes that have been made about the matches described in Reading Passage 1. Decide which type of match (A–H) corresponds with each description and write your answers in boxes 9–15 on your answer sheet.

NB There are more matches than descriptions so you will not use them all. You may use any match more than once.

Example	*Answer*
could be lit after soaking in water	**H**

NOTES

9 made using a less poisonous type of phosphorus

10 identical to a previous type of match

11 caused a deadly illness

12 first to look like modern matches

13 first matches used for advertising

14 relied on an airtight glass container

15 made with the help of an army design

Types of Matches

A   the Ethereal Match

B   the Instantaneous Lightbox

C   Congreves

D   Lucifers

E   the first strike-anywhere match

F   Lundstrom's safety match

G   book matches

H   waterproof matches

READING PASSAGE 2

*You should spend about 20 minutes on **Questions 16–28** which are based on Reading Passage 2 below.*

Zoo conservation programmes

One of London Zoo's recent advertisements caused me some irritation, so patently did it distort reality. Headlined 'Without zoos you might as well tell these animals to get stuffed', it was bordered with illustrations of several endangered species and went on to extol the myth that without zoos like London Zoo these animals 'will almost certainly disappear forever'. With the zoo world's rather mediocre record on conservation, one might be forgiven for being slightly sceptical about such an advertisement.

Zoos were originally created as places of entertainment, and their suggested involvement with conservation didn't seriously arise until about 30 years ago, when the Zoological Society of London held the first formal international meeting on the subject. Eight years later, a series of world conferences took place, entitled 'The Breeding of Endangered Species', and from this point onwards conservation became the zoo community's buzzword. This commitment has now been clearly defined in *The World Zoo Conservation Strategy* (WZCS, September 1993), which – although an important and welcome document – does seem to be based on an unrealistic optimism about the nature of the zoo industry.

The *WZCS* estimates that there are about 10,000 zoos in the world, of which around 1,000 represent a core of quality collections capable of participating in co-ordinated conservation programmes. This is probably the document's first failing, as I believe that 10,000 is a serious underestimate of the total number of places masquerading as zoological establishments. Of course it is difficult to get accurate data but, to put the issue into perspective, I have found that, in a year of working in Eastern Europe, I discover fresh zoos on almost a weekly basis.

The second flaw in the reasoning of the *WZCS* document is the naive faith it places in its 1,000 core zoos. One would assume that the calibre of these institutions would have been carefully examined, but it appears that the criterion for inclusion on this select list might merely be that the zoo is a member of a zoo federation or association. This might be a good starting point, working on the premise that members must meet certain standards, but again the facts don't support the theory. The greatly respected American Association of Zoological Parks and Aquariums (AAZPA) has had extremely dubious members, and in the UK the Federation of Zoological Gardens of Great Britain and Ireland has occasionally had members that have been roundly censured in the national press. These include Robin Hill Adventure Park on the Isle of Wight, which many considered the most notorious collection of animals in the country. This establishment, which for years was protected by the Isle's local council (which viewed it as a tourist amenity), was finally closed down following a damning report by a veterinary inspector appointed under the terms of the Zoo Licensing Act 1981. As it was always a collection of dubious repute, one is obliged to reflect upon the standards that the Zoo Federation sets when granting membership. The situation is even worse in developing countries where little money is available for redevelopment and it is hard to see a way of incorporating collections into the overall scheme of the *WZCS*.

Even assuming that the *WZCS*'s 1,000 core zoos are all of a high standard – complete with scientific staff and research facilities, trained and dedicated keepers, accommodation that permits normal or natural behaviour, and a policy of co-operating fully with one another – what might be the potential for conservation? Colin Tudge, author of *Last Animals at the Zoo* (Oxford University Press, 1992), argues that 'if the world's zoos worked together in co-operative breeding programmes, then even without further expansion they could save around 2,000 species of endangered land vertebrates'. This seems an extremely optimistic proposition from a man who must be aware of the failings and weaknesses of the zoo industry – the man who, when a member of the council of London Zoo, had to persuade the zoo to devote more of its activities to conservation. Moreover, where are the facts to support such optimism?

Today approximately 16 species might be said to have been 'saved' by captive breeding programmes, although a number of these can hardly be looked upon as resounding successes. Beyond that, about a further 20 species are being seriously considered for zoo conservation programmes. Given that the international conference at London Zoo was held 30 years ago, this is pretty slow progress, and a long way off Tudge's target of 2,000.

Questions 16–22

Do the following statements agree with the views of the writer in Reading Passage 2?
In boxes 16–22 write

YES	*if the statement agrees with the writer*
NO	*if the statement contradicts the writer*
NOT GIVEN	*if it is impossible to say what the writer thinks about this*

Example	*Answer*
London Zoo's advertisements are poorly presented.	NOT GIVEN

16 London Zoo's advertisements are dishonest.

17 Zoos made an insignificant contribution to conservation up until 30 years ago.

18 The WZCS document is not known in Eastern Europe.

19 Zoos in the WZCS select list were carefully inspected.

20 No-one knew how the animals were being treated at Robin Hill Adventure Park.

21 Colin Tudge was dissatisfied with the treatment of animals at London Zoo.

22 The number of successful zoo conservation programmes is unsatisfactory.

Questions 23–25

*Choose the appropriate letters **A–D** and write them in boxes 23–25 on your answer sheet.*

23 What were the objectives of the WZCS document?

  A to improve the calibre of zoos world-wide
  B to identify zoos suitable for conservation practice
  C to provide funds for zoos in underdeveloped countries
  D to list the endangered species of the world

24 Why does the writer refer to Robin Hill Adventure Park?

  A to support the Isle of Wight local council
  B to criticise the 1981 Zoo Licensing Act
  C to illustrate a weakness in the WZCS document
  D to exemplify the standards in AAZPA zoos

25 What word best describes the writer's response to Colin Tudges' prediction on captive breeding programmes?

    A   disbelieving
    B   impartial
    C   prejudiced
    D   accepting

Questions 26–28

The writer mentions a number of factors which lead him to doubt the value of the WZCS document. Which **THREE** *of the following factors are mentioned? Write your answers (A–F) in boxes 26–28 on your answer sheet.*

List of Factors

A   the number of unregistered zoos in the world

B   the lack of money in developing countries

C   the actions of the Isle of Wight local council

D   the failure of the WZCS to examine the standards of the 'core zoos'

E   the unrealistic aim of the WZCS in view of the number of species 'saved' to date

F   the policies of WZCS zoo managers

READING PASSAGE 3

*You should spend about 20 minutes on **Questions 29–40** which are based on Reading Passage 3 below.*

ARCHITECTURE – Reaching for the Sky

Architecture is the art and science of designing buildings and structures. A building reflects the scientific and technological achievements of the age as well as the ideas and aspirations of the designer and client. The appearance of individual buildings, however, is often controversial.

The use of an architectural style cannot be said to start or finish on a specific date. Neither is it possible to say exactly what characterises a particular movement. But the origins of what is now generally known as modern architecture can be traced back to the social and technological changes of the 18th and 19th centuries.

Instead of using timber, stone and traditional building techniques, architects began to explore ways of creating buildings by using the latest technology and materials such as steel, glass and concrete strengthened steel bars, known as reinforced concrete. Technological advances also helped bring about the decline of rural industries and an increase in urban populations as people moved to the towns to work in the new factories. Such rapid and uncontrolled growth helped to turn parts of cities into slums.

By the 1920s architects throughout Europe were reacting against the conditions created by industrialisation. A new style of architecture emerged to reflect more idealistic notions for the future. It was made possible by new materials and construction techniques and was known as Modernism.

By the 1930s many buildings emerging from this movement were designed in the International Style. This was largely characterised by the bold use of new materials and simple, geometric forms, often with white walls supported by stilt-like pillars. These were stripped of unnecessary decoration that would detract from their primary purpose – to be used or lived in.

Walter Gropius, Charles Jeanneret (better known as Le Corbusier) and Ludwig Mies van der Rohe were among the most influential of the many architects who contributed to the development of Modernism in the first half of the century. But the economic depression of the 1930s and the second world war (1939–45) prevented their ideas from being widely realised until the economic conditions improved and war-torn cities had to be rebuilt. By the 1950s, the International Style had developed into a universal approach to building, which standardised the appearance of new buildings in cities across the world.

Unfortunately, this Modernist interest in geometric simplicity and function became exploited for profit. The rediscovery of quick-and-easy-to-handle reinforced concrete and an improved ability to prefabricate building sections meant that builders could meet the budgets of commissioning authorities and handle a renewed demand for development quickly and cheaply. But this led to many badly designed buildings, which discredited the original aims of Modernism.

Influenced by Le Corbusier's ideas on town planning, every large British city built multi-storey housing estates in the 1960s. Mass-produced, low-cost high-rises seemed to offer a solution to the problem of housing a growing inner-city population. But far from meeting human needs, the new estates often proved to be windswept deserts lacking essential social facilities and services. Many of these buildings were poorly designed and constructed and have since been demolished.

By the 1970s a new respect for the place of buildings within the existing townscape arose. Preserving historic buildings or keeping only their facades (or fronts) grew common. Architects also began to make more use of building styles and materials that were traditional to the area. The architectural style usually referred to as High-Tech was also emerging. It celebrated scientific and engineering achievements by openly parading the sophisticated techniques used in construction. Such buildings are commonly made of metal and glass; examples are Stansted airport and the Lloyd's building in London.

Disillusionment at the failure of many of the poor imitations of Modernist architecture led to interest in various styles and ideas from the past and present. By the 1980s the coexistence of different styles of architecture in the same building became known as Post-Modern. Other architects looked back to the classical tradition. The trend in architecture now favours smaller scale building design that reflects a growing public awareness of environmental issues such as energy efficiency. Like the Modernists, people today recognise that a well designed environment improves the quality of life but is not necessarily achieved by adopting one well defined style of architecture.

Twentieth century architecture will mainly be remembered for its tall buildings. They have been made possible by the development of light steel frames and safe passenger lifts. They originated in the US over a century ago to help meet the demand for more economical use of land. As construction techniques improved, the skyscraper became a reality.

Ruth Coleman

Questions 29–35

*Complete the table below using information from Reading Passage 3. Write **NO MORE THAN THREE WORDS** for each answer. Write your answers in boxes 29–35 on your answer sheet.*

PERIOD	STYLE OF PERIOD	BUILDING MATERIALS	CHARACTERISTICS
Before 18th century	*Example* traditional	... (29) ...	
1920s	introduction of ... (30) ...	steel, glass and concrete	exploration of latest technology
1930s – 1950s	... (31) ...		geometric forms
1960s	decline of Modernism	pre-fabricated sections	... (32) ...
1970s	end of Modernist era	traditional materials	... (33) ... of historic buildings
1970s	beginning of ... (34) ... era	metal and glass	sophisticated techniques paraded
1980s	Post-Modernism		... (35) ...

Questions 36–40

Reading Passage 3 describes a number of cause and effect relationships. Match each Cause (36–40) in List A, with its Effect (A–H) in List B.

Write your answers (A–H) in boxes 36–40 on your answer sheet.

NB *There are more effects in List B than you will need, so you will not use all of them. You may use any effect more than once if you wish.*

List A CAUSES	List B EFFECTS
36 A rapid movement of people from rural areas to cities is triggered by technological advance.	**A** The quality of life is improved.
	B Architecture reflects the age.
37 Buildings become simple and functional.	**C** A number of these have been knocked down.
38 An economic depression and the second world war hit Europe.	**D** Light steel frames and lifts are developed.
39 Multi-storey housing estates are built according to contemporary ideas on town planning.	**E** Historical buildings are preserved.
	F All decoration is removed.
40 Less land must be used for building.	**G** Parts of cities become slums.
	H Modernist ideas cannot be put into practice until the second half of the 20th century.

WRITING

WRITING TASK 1

You should spend about 20 minutes on this task.

The charts below show the <u>results of a survey of adult education</u>. The first chart shows the <u>reasons why adults decide to study</u>. The pie chart shows how people think the costs of adult education should be shared.

Write a report for a university lecturer, describing the information shown below.

You should write at least 150 words.

Reasons for study

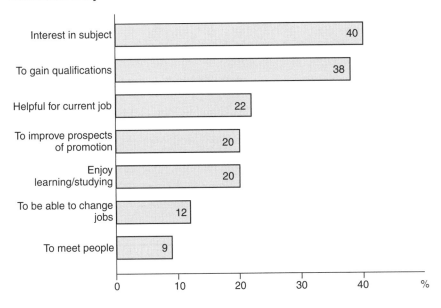

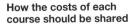

How the costs of each course should be shared

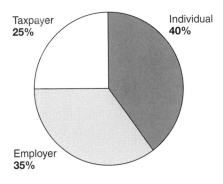

WRITING TASK 2

You should spend about 40 minutes on this task.

Present a written argument or case to an educated reader with no specialist knowledge of the following topic:

> *There are many different types of music in the world today. Why do we need music? Is the traditional music of a country more important than the international music that is heard everywhere nowadays?*

You should write at least 250 words.

Use your own ideas, knowledge and experience and support your arguments with examples and relevant evidence.

SPEAKING

CANDIDATE'S CUE CARD   **Task 1**

UNIVERSITY CLUBS AND ASSOCIATIONS

You have just arrived at a new university. It is orientation week and you want to know about the different clubs and associations you can join. Your examiner is a Student Union representative.

Ask the examiner about: types of clubs
                           meeting times
                           benefits
                           costs

INTERVIEWER'S NOTES

UNIVERSITY CLUBS AND ASSOCIATIONS

Prompts for interviewer

Overseas Students Club
- Meets once a week in Student
  Centre, near Library   *All welcome*

- Helps you to meet other students

- Financial contributions welcome

Chess Club
- Meets once a week in Library   *Not suitable for beginners*

- Plays other universities   *Serious players only*

- No subscription

Table Tennis Club
- Meets every day at lunch-time in
  student area near canteen   *All welcome*

- Arranges tournaments

- $5.00 subscription

Note: A revised Speaking Module will be operational from July 2001. See page 155 for details and sample tasks.

Practice Test 2

SECTION 1   *Questions 1–10*

*Complete the notes. Use **NO MORE THAN THREE WORDS** for each answer.*

KATE	
Her first impressions of the town	*Example* *Quiet*
Type of accommodation	**(1)**
Her feelings about the accommodation	**(2)**
Her feelings about the other students	**(3)**
Name of course	*Environmental Studies*
Difficulties experienced on the course	**(4)**
Suggestions for improving the course	**(5)**

LUKI	
First type of accommodation	**(6)**
Problem with the first accommodation	**(7)**
Second type of accommodation	**(8)**
Name of course	**(9)**
Comments about the course	*Computer room busy*
Suggestions for improving the course	**(10)**

SECTION 2   *Questions 11–20*

Complete the notes below. Use **NO MORE THAN THREE WORDS** *for each answer.*

There are many kinds of bicycles available:

racing
touring
(11) ....
ordinary

They vary in price and **(12)** ....

Prices range from $50.00 to **(13)** ....

Single speed cycles are suitable for **(14)** ....

Three speed cycles are suitable for **(15)** ....

Five and ten speed cycles are suitable for longer distances, hills
and **(16)** ....

Ten speed bikes are better because they are **(17)** .... in
price but **(18)** ....

Buying a cycle is like **(19)** ....

The size of the bicycle is determined by the size of
the **(20)** ....

SECTION 3   *Questions 21–32*

Questions 21–24

Circle the correct answer.

21   At first Fiona thinks that Martin's tutorial topic is

    A   inappropriate.
    B   dull.
    C   interesting.
    D   fascinating.

22   According to Martin, the banana

    A   has only recently been cultivated.
    B   is economical to grow.
    C   is good for your health.
    D   is his favourite food.

23   Fiona listens to Martin because she

    A   wants to know more about bananas.
    B   has nothing else to do today.
    C   is interested in the economy of Australia.
    D   wants to help Martin.

24   According to Martin, bananas were introduced into Australia from

    A   India.
    B   England.
    C   China.
    D   Africa.

Questions 25–30

Complete Martin's notes. Use **NO MORE THAN THREE WORDS** *for each answer.*

Commercially grown
banana plant

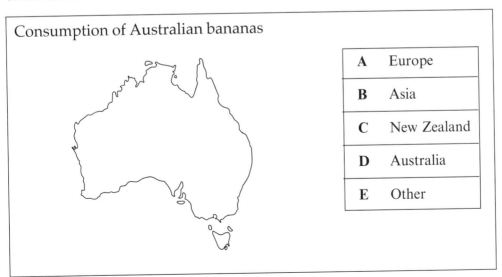

Each banana tree produces
(25) ....
of bananas.

On modern plantations in tropical
conditions a tree can bear fruit after
(26) ....

Banana trees prefer to grow **(27)** .... and they require
rich soil and **(28)** .... The fruit is often protected by
(29) ....

Ripe bananas emit a gas which helps other **(30)** ....

Questions 31 and 32

Circle the **TWO** *correct boxes.*

Consumption of Australian bananas

A	Europe
B	Asia
C	New Zealand
D	Australia
E	Other

SECTION 4   *Questions 33–41*

Questions 33–35

Circle the correct answer.

According to the first speaker:

33   The focus of the lecture series is on

A	organising work and study.	**C**	coping with homesickness.
B	maintaining a healthy lifestyle.	**D**	settling in at university.

34   The lecture will be given by

A	the president of the Union.	**C**	a sports celebrity.
B	the campus doctor.	**D**	a health expert.

According to the second speaker:

35   This week's lecture is on

A	campus food.	**C**	sensible eating.
B	dieting.	**D**	saving money.

Questions 36–39

*Complete the notes. Write **NO MORE THAN THREE WORDS** for each answer.*

A balanced diet

A balanced diet will give you enough vitamins for normal daily living.
Vitamins in food can be lost through **(36)** ....

Types of vitamins:

(a) Fat soluble vitamins are stored by the body.
(b) Water soluble vitamins – not stored, so you need
    a **(37)** ....

Getting enough vitamins

Eat **(38)** .... of foods.
Buy plenty of vegetables and store them in
(39) ....

Questions 40–41

Complete the diagram by writing **NO MORE THAN THREE WORDS** *in the boxes provided.*

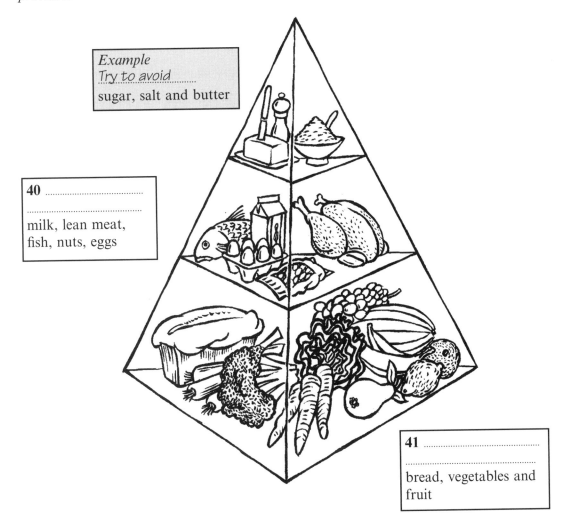

Example
Try to avoid
sugar, salt and butter

40 ....
....
milk, lean meat,
fish, nuts, eggs

41 ....
....
bread, vegetables and
fruit

READING

READING PASSAGE 1

*You should spend about 20 minutes on **Questions 1–12** which are based on Reading Passage 1 below.*

Right and left-handedness in humans

Why do humans, virtually alone among all animal species, display a distinct left or right-handedness? Not even our closest relatives among the apes possess such decided lateral asymmetry, as psychologists call it. Yet about 90 per cent of every human population that has ever lived appears to have been right-handed. Professor Bryan Turner at Deakin University has studied the research literature on left-handedness and found that handedness goes with sidedness. So nine out of ten people are right-handed and eight are right-footed. He noted that this distinctive asymmetry in the human population is itself systematic. 'Humans think in categories: black and white, up and down, left and right. It's a system of signs that enables us to categorise phenomena that are essentially ambiguous.'

Research has shown that there is a genetic or inherited element to handedness. But while left-handedness tends to run in families, neither left nor right handers will automatically produce off-spring with the same handedness; in fact about 6 per cent of children with two right-handed parents will be left-handed. However, among two left-handed parents, perhaps 40 per cent of the children will also be left-handed. With one right and one left-handed parent, 15 to 20 per cent of the offspring will be left-handed. Even among identical twins who have exactly the same genes, one in six pairs will differ in their handedness.

What then makes people left-handed if it is not simply genetic? Other factors must be at work and researchers have turned to the brain for clues. In the 1860s the French surgeon and anthropologist, Dr Paul Broca, made the remarkable finding that patients who had lost their powers of speech as a result of a stroke (a blood clot in the brain) had paralysis of the right half of their body. He noted that since the left hemisphere of the brain controls the right half of the body, and vice versa, the brain damage must have been in the brain's left hemisphere. Psychologists now believe that among right-handed people, probably 95 per cent have their language centre in the left hemisphere, while 5 per cent have right-sided language. Left-handers, however, do not show the reverse pattern but instead a majority also have their language in the left hemisphere. Some 30 per cent have right hemisphere language.

Dr Brinkman, a brain researcher at the Australian National University in Canberra, has suggested that evolution of speech went with right-handed preference. According to Brinkman, as the brain evolved, one side became specialised for fine control of movement (necessary for producing speech) and along with this evolution came right-hand preference. According to Brinkman, most left-handers have left hemisphere dominance but also some capacity in the right hemisphere. She has observed that if a left-handed person is brain-damaged in the left hemisphere, the recovery of speech is quite often better and this is explained by the fact that left-handers have a more bilateral speech function.

In her studies of macaque monkeys, Brinkman has noticed that primates (monkeys) seem to learn a hand preference from their mother in the first year of life but this could be one hand or the other. In humans, however, the specialisation in function of the two hemispheres results in anatomical differences: areas that are involved with the production of speech are usually larger on the left side than on the right. Since monkeys have not acquired the art of speech, one would not expect to see such a variation but Brinkman claims to have discovered a trend in monkeys towards the asymmetry that is evident in the human brain.

Two American researchers, Geschwind and Galaburda, studied the brains of human embryos and discovered that the left-right asymmetry exists before birth. But as the brain develops, a number of things can affect it. Every brain is initially female in its organisation and it only becomes a male brain when the male foetus begins to secrete hormones. Geschwind and Galaburda knew that different parts of the brain mature at different rates; the right hemisphere develops first, then the left. Moreover, a girl's brain develops somewhat faster than that of a boy. So, if something happens to the brain's development during pregnancy, it is more likely to be affected in a male and the hemisphere more likely to be involved is the left. The brain may become less lateralised and this in turn could result in left-handedness and the development of certain superior skills that have their origins in the left hemisphere such as logic, rationality and abstraction. It should be no surprise then that among mathematicians and architects, left-handers tend to be more common and there are more left-handed males than females.

The results of this research may be some consolation to left-handers who have for centuries lived in a world designed to suit right-handed people. However, what is alarming, according to Mr Charles Moore, a writer and journalist, is the way the word 'right' reinforces its own virtue. Subliminally he says, language tells people to think that anything on the right can be trusted while anything on the left is dangerous or even sinister. We speak of left-handed compliments and according to Moore, 'it is no coincidence that left-handed children, forced to use their right hand, often develop a stammer as they are robbed of their freedom of speech'. However, as more research is undertaken on the causes of left-handedness, attitudes towards left-handed people are gradually changing for the better. Indeed when the champion tennis player Ivan Lendl was asked what the single thing was that he would choose in order to improve his game, he said he would like to become a left-hander.

Geoff Maslen

41

Questions 1–7

*Use the information in the text to match the people (listed **A–E**) with the opinions (listed 1–7) below. Write the appropriate letter (**A–E**) in boxes 1–7 on your answer sheet. Some people match more than one opinion.*

A	Dr Broca
B	Dr Brinkman
C	Geschwind and Galaburda
D	Charles Moore
E	Professor Turner

Example	Answer
Monkeys do not show a species specific preference for left or right-handedness.	**B**

1   Human beings started to show a preference for right-handedness when they first developed language.

2   Society is prejudiced against left-handed people.

3   Boys are more likely to be left-handed.

4   After a stroke, left-handed people recover their speech more quickly than right-handed people.

5   People who suffer strokes on the left side of the brain usually lose their power of speech.

6   The two sides of the brain develop different functions before birth.

7   Asymmetry is a common feature of the human body.

Questions 8–10

Using the information in the passage, complete the table below. Write your answers in boxes 8–10 on your answer sheet.

	Percentage of children left-handed
One parent left-handed One parent right-handed	... **(8)** ...
Both parents left-handed	... **(9)** ...
Both parents right-handed	... **(10)** ...

Questions 11–12

*Choose the appropriate letters **A–D** and write them in boxes 11 and 12 on your answer sheet.*

11 A study of monkeys has shown that

A monkeys are not usually right-handed.
B monkeys display a capacity for speech.
C monkey brains are smaller than human brains.
D monkey brains are asymmetric.

12 According to the writer, left-handed people

A will often develop a stammer.
B have undergone hardship for years.
C are untrustworthy.
D are good tennis players.

READING PASSAGE 2

*You should spend about 20 minutes on **Questions 13–27** which are based on Reading Passage 2 below.*

MIGRATORY BEEKEEPING

Taking Wing

To eke out a full-time living from their honeybees, about half the nation's 2,000 commercial beekeepers pull up stakes each spring, migrating north to find more flowers for their bees. Besides turning floral nectar into honey, these hardworking insects also pollinate crops for farmers – for a fee. As autumn approaches, the beekeepers pack up their hives and go south, scrambling for pollination contracts in hot spots like California's fertile Central Valley.

Of the 2,000 commercial beekeepers in the United States about half migrate. This pays off in two ways. Moving north in the summer and south in the winter lets bees work a longer blooming season, making more honey – and money – for their keepers. Second, beekeepers can carry their hives to farmers who need bees to pollinate their crops. Every spring a migratory beekeeper in California may move up to 160 million bees to flowering fields in Minnesota and every winter his family may haul the hives back to California, where farmers will rent the bees to pollinate almond and cherry trees.

Migratory beekeeping is nothing new. The ancient Egyptians moved clay hives, probably on rafts, down the Nile to follow the bloom and nectar flow as it moved toward Cairo. In the 1880s North American beekeepers experimented with the same idea, moving bees on barges along the Mississippi and on waterways in Florida, but their lighter, wooden hives kept falling into the water. Other keepers tried the railroad and horse-drawn wagons, but that didn't prove practical. Not until the 1920s when cars and trucks became affordable and roads improved, did migratory beekeeping begin to catch on.

For the Californian beekeeper, the pollination season begins in February. At this time, the beehives are in particular demand by farmers who have almond groves; they need two hives an acre. For the three-week long bloom, beekeepers can hire out their hives for $32 each. It's a bonanza for the bees too. Most people consider almond honey too bitter to eat so the bees get to keep it for themselves.

By early March it is time to move the bees. It can take up to seven nights to pack the 4,000 or so hives that a beekeeper may own. These are not moved in the middle of the day because too many of the bees would end up homeless. But at night, the hives are stacked onto wooden pallets, back-to-back in sets of four, and lifted onto a truck. It is not necessary to wear gloves or a beekeeper's veil because the hives are not being opened and the bees should remain relatively quiet. Just in case some are still lively, bees can be pacified with a few puffs of smoke blown into each hive's narrow entrance.

In their new location, the beekeeper will pay the farmer to allow his bees to feed in such places as orange groves. The honey produced here is fragrant and sweet and can be sold by the beekeepers. To encourage the bees to produce as much honey as possible during this period, the beekeepers open the hives and stack extra boxes called *supers* on top. These temporary hive extensions contain frames of empty comb for the bees to fill with honey. In the brood chamber below, the bees will stash honey to eat later. To prevent the queen from crawling up to the top and laying eggs, a screen can be inserted between the brood chamber and the supers. Three weeks later the honey can be gathered.

Foul smelling chemicals are often used to irritate the bees and drive them down into the hive's bottom boxes, leaving the honey-filled supers more or less bee free. These can then be pulled off the hive. They are heavy with honey and may weigh up to 90 pounds each. The supers are taken to a warehouse. In the extracting room, the frames are lifted out and lowered into an 'uncapper' where rotating blades shave away the wax that covers each cell. The uncapped frames are put in a carousel that sits on the bottom of a large stainless steel drum. The carousel is filled to capacity with 72 frames. A switch is flipped and the frames begin to whirl at 300 revolutions per minute; centrifugal force throws the honey out of the combs. Finally the honey is poured into barrels for shipment.

After this, approximately a quarter of the hives weakened by disease, mites, or an ageing or dead queen, will have to be replaced. To create new colonies, a healthy double hive, teeming with bees, can be separated into two boxes. One half will hold the queen and a young, already mated queen can be put in the other half, to make two hives from one. By the time the flowers bloom, the new queens will be laying eggs, filling each hive with young worker bees. The beekeeper's family will then migrate with them to their summer location.

Adapted from 'America's Beekeepers: Hives for Hire' by Alan Mairson, National Geographic.

Questions 13–19

The flow chart below outlines the movements of the migratory beekeeper as described in Reading Passage 2.
Complete the flow chart. Choose your answers from the box at the bottom of the page and write your answers in boxes 13–19 on your answer sheet.

BEEKEEPER MOVEMENTS

> *Example*   *Answer*
> In February, Californian farmers hire bees to help ..*pollinate*... almond trees.

↓

In March, beekeepers ... **(13)** ... for migration at night when the hives are ... **(14)** ... and the bees are generally tranquil. A little ... **(15)** ... can ensure that this is the case.

↓

They transport their hives to orange groves where farmers .... **(16)** ... beekeepers for placing them on their land. Here the bees make honey.

↓

After three weeks, the supers can be taken to a warehouse where ... **(17)** ... are used to remove the wax and extract the honey from the ... **(18)** ... .

↓

After the honey collection, the old hives are rejected. Good double hives are ... **(19)** ... and re-queened and the beekeeper transports them to their summer base.

List of Words/Phrases

smoke	chemicals	pay
barrels	protection	charge
~~set off~~	light	split
~~pollinate~~	machines	supers
combs	screen	prepare
full	empty	queens

Questions 20–23

*Label the diagram below. Choose **ONE OR TWO WORDS** from the Reading Passage for each answer. Write your answers in boxes 20–23 on your answer sheet.*

A BEEHIVE

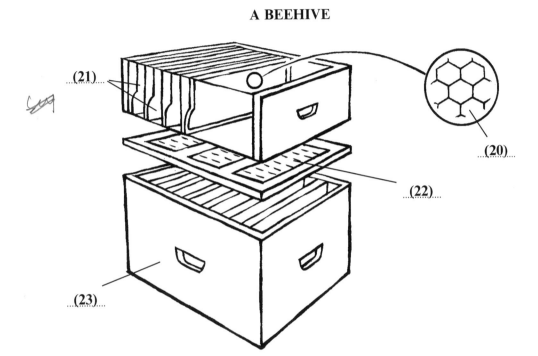

Questions 24–27

Do the following statements agree with the information given in Reading Passage 2?
In boxes 24–27 write

    YES   *if the statement agrees with the information given*
    NO   *if the statement contradicts the information given*
    NOT GIVEN *if there is no information about this*

24   The Egyptians keep bees on the banks of the Nile.

25   First attempts at migratory beekeeping in America were unsuccessful.

26   Bees keep honey for themselves in the bottom of the hive.

27   The honey is spun to make it liquid.

READING PASSAGE 3

*You should spend about 20 minutes on **Questions 28–41** which are based on Reading Passage 3 below.*

TOURISM

A Tourism, holidaymaking and travel are these days more significant social phenomena than most commentators have considered. On the face of it there could not be a more trivial subject for a book. And indeed since social scientists have had considerable difficulty explaining weightier topics, such as work or politics, it might be thought that they would have great difficulties in accounting for more trivial phenomena such as holidaymaking. However, there are interesting parallels with the study of deviance. This involves the investigation of bizarre and idiosyncratic social practices which happen to be defined as deviant in some societies but not necessarily in others. The assumption is that the investigation of deviance can reveal interesting and significant aspects of 'normal' societies. It could be said that a similar analysis can be applied to tourism.

B Tourism is a leisure activity which presupposes its opposite, namely regulated and organised work. It is one manifestation of how work and leisure are organised as separate and regulated spheres of social practice in 'modern' societies. Indeed acting as a tourist is one of the defining characteristics of being 'modern' and the popular concept of tourism is that it is organised within particular places and occurs for regularised periods of time. Tourist relationships arise from a movement of people to, and their stay in, various destinations. This necessarily involves some movement, that is the journey, and a period of stay in a new place or places. The journey and the stay are by definition outside the normal places of residence and work and are of a short-term and temporary nature and there is a clear intention to return 'home' within a relatively short period of time.

C A substantial proportion of the population of modern societies engages in such tourist practices; new socialised forms of provision have developed in order to cope with the mass character of the gazes of tourists, as opposed to the individual character of travel. Places are chosen to be visited and be gazed upon because there is an anticipation, especially through daydreaming and fantasy, of intense pleasures, either on a different scale or involving different senses from those customarily encountered. Such anticipation is constructed and sustained through a variety of non-tourist practices, such as films, TV, literature, magazines, records and videos which construct and reinforce this daydreaming.

D Tourists tend to visit features of landscape and townscape which separate them off from everyday experience. Such aspects are viewed because they are taken to be in some sense out of the ordinary. The viewing of these tourist sights often involves different forms of social patterning, with a much greater sensitivity to visual elements of landscape or townscape than is normally found in everyday life. People linger over these sights in a way that they would not normally do in their home environment and the vision is objectified or captured through photographs, postcards, films and so on which enable the memory to be endlessly reproduced and recaptured.

E One of the earliest dissertations on the subject of tourism is Boorstin's analysis of the 'pseudo-event' (1964) where he argues that contemporary Americans cannot experience 'reality' directly but thrive on 'pseudo-events'. Isolated from the host environment and the local people, the mass tourist travels in guided groups and finds pleasure in inauthentic contrived attractions, gullibly enjoying the pseudo-events and disregarding the real world outside. Over time the images generated of different tourist sights come to constitute a closed self-perpetuating system of illusions which provide the tourist with the basis for selecting and evaluating potential places to visit. Such visits are made, says

Boorstin, within the 'environmental bubble' of the familiar American-style hotel which insulates the tourist from the strangeness of the host environment.

F To service the burgeoning tourist industry, an array of professionals has developed who attempt to reproduce ever-new objects for the tourist to look at. These objects or places are located in a complex and changing hierarchy. This depends upon the interplay between, on the one hand, competition between interests involved in the provision of such objects and, on the other hand, changing class, gender, and generational distinctions of taste within the potential population of visitors. It has been said that to be a tourist is one of the characteristics of the 'modern experience'. Not to 'go away' is like not possessing a car or a nice house. Travel is a marker of status in modern societies and is also thought to be necessary for good health. The role of the professional, therefore, is to cater for the needs and tastes of the tourists in accordance with their class and overall expectations.

Questions 28–32

*Reading Passage 3 has 6 paragraphs (**A–F**). Choose the most suitable heading for each paragraph from the list of headings below. Write the appropriate numbers (**i–ix**) in boxes 28–32 on your answer sheet. Paragraph D has been done for you as an example.*

NB *There are more headings than paragraphs so you will not use all of them. You may use any heading more than once.*

List of Headings
i The politics of tourism
ii The cost of tourism
iii Justifying the study of tourism
iv Tourism contrasted with travel
v The essence of modern tourism
vi Tourism *versus* leisure
vii The artificiality of modern tourism
viii The role of modern tour guides
ix ~~Creating an alternative to the everyday experience~~

28 Paragraph A

29 Paragraph B

30 Paragraph C

Example	*Answer*
Paragraph D	**ix**

31 Paragraph E

32 Paragraph F

Questions 33–37

Do the following statements agree with the views of the writer in Reading Passage 3?
In boxes 33–37 write

> **YES**   *if the statement agrees with the writer*
> **NO**   *if the statement contradicts the writer*
> **NOT GIVEN** *if it is impossible to say what the writer thinks about this*

Example	*Answer*
People who can't afford to travel watch films and TV.	**NOT GIVEN**

33   Tourism is a trivial subject.

34   An analysis of deviance can act as a model for the analysis of tourism.

35   Tourists usually choose to travel overseas.

36   Tourists focus more on places they visit than those at home.

37   Tour operators try to cheat tourists.

Questions 38–41

*Choose one phrase (**A–H**) from the list of phrases to complete each key point below. Write the appropriate letters (**A–H**) in boxes 38–41 on your answer sheet.*

The information in the completed sentences should be an accurate summary of points made by the writer.

*NB   There are more phrases **A–H** than sentences so you will not use them all.*
You may use any phrase more than once.

38   Our concept of tourism arises from ...

39   The media can be used to enhance ...

40   People view tourist landscapes in a different way from ...

41   Group tours encourage participants to look at ...

List of Phrases

A	local people and their environment.	**E**	the individual character of travel.
B	the expectations of tourists.	**F**	places seen in everyday life.
C	the phenomena of holidaymaking.	**G**	photographs which recapture our holidays.
D	the distinction we make between work and leisure.	**H**	sights designed specially for tourists.

WRITING

WRITING TASK 1

You should spend about 20 minutes on this task.

The diagram below shows how the Australian Bureau of Meteorology collects up-to-the-minute information on the weather in order to produce reliable forecasts.

Write a report for a university lecturer describing the information shown below.

You should write at least 150 words.

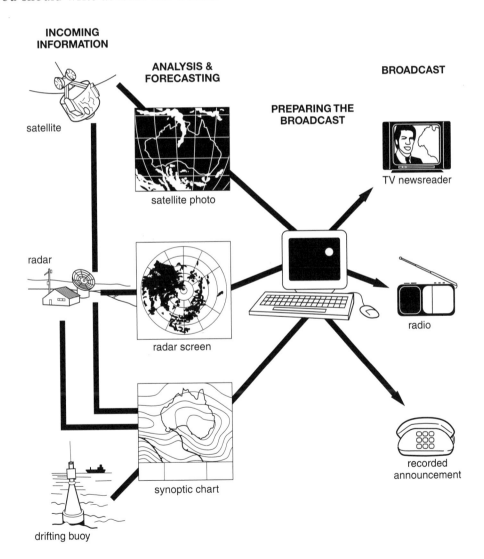

INCOMING INFORMATION

satellite

radar

drifting buoy

ANALYSIS & FORECASTING

satellite photo

radar screen

synoptic chart

PREPARING THE BROADCAST

BROADCAST

TV newsreader

radio

recorded announcement

WRITING TASK 2

You should spend about 40 minutes on this task.

Present a written argument or case to an educated reader with no specialist knowledge of the following topic.

> *Should wealthy nations be required to share their wealth among poorer nations by providing such things as food and education? Or is it the responsibility of the governments of poorer nations to look after their citizens themselves?*

You should write at least 250 words.

Use your own ideas, knowledge and experience and support your arguments with examples and with relevant evidence.

SPEAKING

CANDIDATE'S CUE CARD   **Task 2**

ASKING FOR AN EXTENSION

You have to give in a piece of work to your lecturer next Wednesday. You need two more weeks to prepare the assignment because you have had difficulty obtaining the reference books. Your examiner is your lecturer. Find out if you can have an extension.

Ask the examiner about: regulations regarding late work
possibility of having more time
different sources for books/information
assistance with writing for overseas students

INTERVIEWER'S NOTES

ASKING FOR AN EXTENSION

The student is seeking extra time for an assignment.

• The student may need to write a letter.

• The student has had plenty of time to prepare the work and should not really need two more weeks.

• Provide some idea about where he/she may get hold of the books.

• Offer advice about the 'Learning Assistance Centre' on the campus which helps students with essay writing.

After some resistance, agree to an extension of one week.

Note: A revised Speaking Module will be operational from July 2001. See page 155 for details and sample tasks.

Practice Test 3

SECTION 1   *Questions 1–12*

Questions 1–4

Circle the appropriate letter.

Example

How does the woman travel every day?

A   by car
B   by bus
C   on foot
D   by train

---

1   What are the parking regulations on campus?

    A   undergraduate parking allowed
    B   postgraduate parking allowed
    C   staff parking only allowed
    D   no student parking allowed

2   The administration office is in

    A   Block B.
    B   Block D.
    C   Block E.
    D   Block G.

3   If you do not have a parking sticker, the following action will be taken:

    A   wheel clamp your car.
    B   fine only.
    C   tow away your car and fine.
    D   tow away your car only.

4   Which picture shows the correct location of the Administration office?

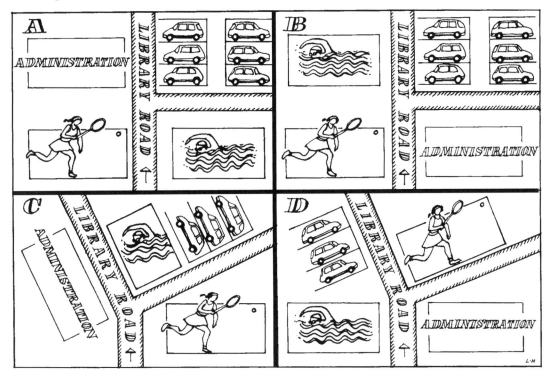

Questions 5–10

Complete the application form using **NO MORE THAN THREE WORDS**.

Application for parking sticker

Name   **(5)** ....

Address   **(6) Flat 13** ....

Suburb   **(7)** ....

Faculty   **(8)** ....

Registration number   **(9)** ....

Make of car   **(10)** ....

Questions 11–12

11   Cashier's office opens at   **A**   12.15   **B**   2.00   **C**   2.15   **D**   4.30

12   Where must the sticker be displayed? ....

SECTION 2   *Questions 13–23*

*Complete the notes below using **NO MORE THAN THREE WORDS** for each answer.*

Date the museum was opened	**(13)**
The museum consists of a building and	**(14)**
Handicapped toilet door shows	*Example* **a wheelchair**
The Education Centre is signposted by	**(15)**
If you lose your friends, meet at the	**(16)**
Warning about *The Vampire*	**(17)**
How often are the tours of *The Vampire*?	**(18)**
Person featured in today's video	**(19)**
The Leisure Gallery shows how Australian culture is influenced by	**(20)**
The Picture Gallery contains pictures by	**(21)**
Cost of family membership of the museum	**(22)**
'Passengers and the Sea' includes a collection of	**(23)**

SECTION 3   *Questions 24–32*

Questions 24–27

Circle the correct answer.

24 Mark is going to talk briefly about

    A marketing new products.
    B pricing strategies.
    C managing large companies.
    D setting sales targets.

25 According to Susan, air fares are lowest when they

    A include weekend travel.
    B are booked well in advance.
    C are non-refundable.
    D are for business travel only.

26 Mark thinks revenue management is

    A interesting.
    B complicated.
    C time-consuming.
    D reasonable.

27 The airline companies want to

    A increase profits.
    B benefit the passenger.
    C sell cheap seats.
    D improve the service.

Questions 28–32

*Complete the notes using **NO MORE THAN THREE WORDS** for each answer.*

Two reasons for the new approach to pricing are:

(28) .... and

(29) ....

In future people will be able to book airline tickets **(30)** ....

Also being marketed in this way are **(31)** .... and

(32) ....

SECTION 4   *Questions 33–42*

Questions 33–37

Complete the table. Write NO MORE THAN THREE WORDS for each answer.

SPACE MANAGEMENT

RESEARCH METHOD	INFORMATION PROVIDED
Questionnaires	what customers think about (33) ....
(34)	how customers move around supermarket aisles
Eye movement (35)	the most eye-catching areas of the shop
Computer programs e.g. (36)	the best (37) .... for an article in the shop

Questions 38–42

Label the diagram. Write **NO MORE THAN THREE WORDS** *for each answer.*

A SUPERMARKET AISLE

ENTRANCE

First shelves –
customers usually
(38) ....
these.

EXIT

Checkout – often
used to sell
(42) ....

....

AISLE

← Products placed here
sell well particularly
if they are placed
(39) ....

....

→

← These areas are
known as
(40) ....

....

→

Gondola end –
prime position:
used to launch
launch new
products

Gondola end –
often find
(41) ....

....

displayed here.

READING

READING PASSAGE 1

*You should spend about 20 minutes on **Questions 1–12** which are based on Reading Passage 1 below.*

SPOKEN CORPUS COMES TO LIFE

A The compiling of dictionaries has been historically the provenance of studious professorial types – usually bespectacled – who love to pore over weighty tomes and make pronouncements on the finer nuances of meaning. They were probably good at crosswords and definitely knew a lot of words, but the image was always rather dry and dusty. The latest technology, and simple technology at that, is revolutionising the content of dictionaries and the way they are put together.

B For the first time, dictionary publishers are incorporating real, spoken English into their data. It gives lexicographers (people who write dictionaries) access to a more vibrant, up-to-date vernacular language which has never really been studied before. In one project, 150 volunteers each agreed to discreetly tie a Walkman recorder to their waist and leave it running for anything up to two weeks. Every conversation they had was recorded. When the data was collected, the length of tapes was 35 times the depth of the Atlantic Ocean. Teams of audio typists transcribed the tapes to produce a computerised database of ten million words.

C This has been the basis – along with an existing written corpus – for the Language Activator dictionary, described by lexicographer Professor Randolph Quirk as 'the book the world has been waiting for'. It shows advanced foreign learners of English how the language is really used. In the dictionary, key words such as 'eat' are followed by related phrases such as 'wolf down' or 'be a picky eater', allowing the student to choose the appropriate phrase.

D 'This kind of research would be impossible without computers,' said Della Summers, a director of dictionaries. 'It has transformed the way lexicographers work. If you look at the word 'like', you may intuitively think that the first and most frequent meaning is the verb, as in 'I like swimming'. It is not. It is the preposition, as in: 'she walked like a duck'. Just because a word or phrase is used doesn't mean it ends up in a dictionary. The sifting out process is as vital as ever. But the database does allow lexicographers to search for a word and find out how frequently it is used – something that could only be guessed at intuitively before.

E   Researchers have found that written English works in a very different way to spoken English. The phrase 'say what you like' literally means 'feel free to say anything you want', but in reality it is used, evidence shows, by someone to prevent the other person voicing disagreement. The phrase 'it's a question of' crops up on the database over and over again. It has nothing to do with enquiry, but it's one of the most frequent English phrases which has never been in a language learner's dictionary before: it is now.

F   The Spoken Corpus computer shows how inventive and humorous people are when they are using language by twisting familiar phrases for effect. It also reveals the power of the pauses and noises we use to play for time, convey emotion, doubt and irony.

G   For the moment, those benefiting most from the Spoken Corpus are foreign learners. 'Computers allow lexicographers to search quickly through more examples of real English,' said Professor Geoffrey Leech of Lancaster University. 'They allow dictionaries to be more accurate and give a feel for how language is being used.' The Spoken Corpus is part of the larger British National Corpus, an initiative carried out by several groups involved in the production of language learning materials: publishers, universities and the British Library.

Questions 1–6

Reading Passage 1 has seven paragraphs (A–G). Choose the most suitable heading for each paragraph from the list of headings below. Write the appropriate numbers (i–xi) in boxes 1–6 on your answer sheet. Paragraph C has been done for you as an example.

NB   *There are more headings than paragraphs so you will not use all of them. You may use any heading more than once.*

List of Headings

i	Grammar is corrected
ii	New method of research
iii	Technology learns from dictionaries
iv	Non-verbal content
v	The first study of spoken language
vi	Traditional lexicographical methods
vii	Written English tells the truth
viii	New phrases enter dictionary
ix	A cooperative research project
x	Accurate word frequency counts
xi	Alternative expressions provided

---

1   Paragraph A

2   Paragraph B

Example	*Answer*
Paragraph C	**xi**

3   Paragraph D

4   Paragraph E

5   Paragraph F

6   Paragraph G

Questions 7–11

*The diagram below illustrates the information provided in paragraphs **B–F** of Reading Passage 1. Complete the labels on the diagram with an appropriate word or words. Use **NO MORE THAN THREE WORDS** for each space. Write your answers in boxes 7–11 on your answer sheet.*

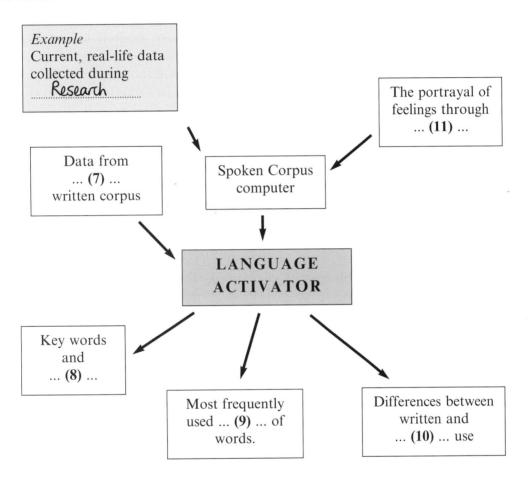

*Choose the appropriate letter **A–D** and write it in box 12 on your answer sheet.*

12   Why was this article written?

   A   To give an example of a current dictionary.
   B   To announce a new approach to dictionary writing.
   C   To show how dictionaries have progressed over the years.
   D   To compare the content of different dictionaries.

READING PASSAGE 2

*You should spend about 20 minutes on **Questions 13–26** which are based on Reading Passage 2 below.*

Moles happy as homes go underground

A The first anybody knew about Dutchman Frank Siegmund and his family was when workmen tramping through a field found a narrow steel chimney protruding through the grass. Closer inspection revealed a chink of sky-light window among the thistles, and when amazed investigators moved down the side of the hill they came across a pine door complete with leaded diamond glass and a brass knocker set into an underground building. The Siegmunds had managed to live undetected for six years outside the border town of Breda, in Holland. They are the latest in a clutch of individualistic homemakers who have burrowed underground in search of tranquillity.

B Most, falling foul of strict building regulations, have been forced to dismantle their individualistic homes and return to more conventional lifestyles. But subterranean suburbia, Dutch-style, is about to become respectable and chic. Seven luxury homes cosseted away inside a high earth-covered noise embankment next to the main Tilburg city road recently went on the market for $296,500 each. The foundations had yet to be dug, but customers queued up to buy the unusual part-submerged houses, whose back wall consists of a grassy mound and whose front is a long glass gallery.

C The Dutch are not the only would-be moles. Growing numbers of Europeans are burrowing below ground to create houses, offices, discos and shopping malls. It is already proving a way of life in extreme climates; in winter months in Montreal, Canada, for instance, citizens can escape the cold in an underground complex complete with shops and even health clinics. In Tokyo builders are planning a massive underground city to be begun in the next decade, and underground shopping malls are already common in Japan, where 90 percent of the population is squeezed into 20 percent of the landspace.

D Building big commercial buildings underground can be a way to avoid disfiguring or threatening a beautiful or 'environmentally sensitive' landscape. Indeed many of the buildings which consume most land – such as cinemas, supermarkets, theatres, warehouses or libraries – have no need to be on the surface since they do not need windows.

E There are big advantages, too, when it comes to private homes. A development of 194 houses which would take up 14 hectares of land above ground would occupy 2.7 hectares below it, while the number of roads would be halved. Under several metres of earth, noise is minimal and insulation is excellent. 'We get 40 to 50 enquiries a week,' says Peter Carpenter, secretary of the British Earth Sheltering Association, which builds similar homes in Britain. 'People see this as a way of building for the future.' An underground dweller himself, Carpenter has never paid a heating bill, thanks to solar panels and natural insulation.

F   In Europe, the obstacle has been conservative local authorities and developers who prefer to ensure quick sales with conventional mass-produced housing. But the Dutch development was greeted with undisguised relief by South Limburg planners because of Holland's chronic shortage of land. It was the Tilburg architect Jo Hurkmans who hit on the idea of making use of noise embankments on main roads. His two-floored, four-bedroomed, two-bathroomed detached homes are now taking shape. 'They are not so much below the earth as in it,' he says. 'All the light will come through the glass front, which runs from the second floor ceiling to the ground. Areas which do not need much natural lighting are at the back. The living accommodation is to the front so nobody notices that the back is dark.'

G   In the US, where energy-efficient homes became popular after the oil crisis of 1973, 10,000 underground houses have been built. A terrace of five homes, Britain's first subterranean development, is under way in Nottinghamshire. Italy's outstanding example of subterranean architecture is the Olivetti residential centre in Ivrea. Commissioned by Roberto Olivetti in 1969, it comprises 82 one-bedroomed apartments and 12 maisonettes and forms a house/hotel for Olivetti employees. It is built into a hill and little can be seen from outside except a glass facade. Patrizia Vallecchi, a resident since 1992, says it is little different from living in a conventional apartment.

H   Not everyone adapts so well, and in Japan scientists at the Shimizu Corporation have developed 'space creation' systems which mix light, sounds, breezes and scents to stimulate people who spend long periods below ground. Underground offices in Japan are being equipped with 'virtual' windows and mirrors, while underground departments in the University of Minnesota have periscopes to reflect views and light.

I   But Frank Siegmund and his family love their hobbit lifestyle. Their home evolved when he dug a cool room for his bakery business in a hill he had created. During a heatwave they took to sleeping there. 'We felt at peace and so close to nature,' he says. 'Gradually I began adding to the rooms. It sounds strange but we are so close to the earth we draw strength from its vibrations. Our children love it; not every child can boast of being watched through their playroom windows by rabbits.'

Questions 13–20

Reading Passage 2 has nine paragraphs (A–I). Choose the most suitable heading for each paragraph from the list of headings below. Write the appropriate numbers (i–xii) in boxes 13–20 on your answer sheet. Paragraph A has been done for you as an example.

NB   There are more headings than paragraphs so you will not use all of them.

List of Headings

i	A designer describes his houses
ii	Most people prefer conventional housing
iii	Simulating a natural environment
iv	How an underground family home developed
v	Demands on space and energy are reduced
vi	The plans for future homes
vii	Worldwide examples of underground living accommodation
viii	Some buildings do not require natural light
ix	Developing underground services around the world
x	Underground living improves health
xi	Homes sold before completion
xii	An underground home is discovered

Example	*Answer*
Paragraph A	**xii**

---

13   Paragraph B

14   Paragraph C

15   Paragraph D

16   Paragraph E

17   Paragraph F

18   Paragraph G

19   Paragraph H

20   Paragraph I

Questions 21–26

*Complete the sentences below with words taken from the reading passage. Use **NO MORE THAN THREE WORDS** for each answer. Write your answers in boxes 21–26 on your answer sheet.*

21   Many developers prefer mass-produced houses because they ...

22   The Dutch development was welcomed by ...

23   Hurkmans' houses are built into ...

24   The Ivrea centre was developed for ...

25   Japanese scientists are helping people ... underground life.

26   Frank Siegmund's first underground room was used for ...

READING PASSAGE 3

*You should spend about 20 minutes on **Questions 27–38** which are based on Reading Passage 3 below.*

A Workaholic Economy

FOR THE first century or so of the industrial revolution, increased productivity led to decreases in working hours. Employees who had been putting in 12-hour days, six days a week, found their time on the job shrinking to 10 hours daily, then, finally, to eight hours, five days a week. Only a generation ago social planners worried about what people would do with all this new-found free time. In the US, at least, it seems they need not have bothered.

Although the output per hour of work has more than doubled since 1945, leisure seems reserved largely for the unemployed and underemployed. Those who work full-time spend as much time on the job as they did at the end of World War II. In fact, working hours have increased noticeably since 1970 – perhaps because real wages have stagnated since that year. Bookstores now abound with manuals describing how to manage time and cope with stress.

There are several reasons for lost leisure. Since 1979, companies have responded to improvements in the business climate by having employees work overtime rather than by hiring extra personnel, says economist Juliet B. Schor of Harvard University. Indeed, the current economic recovery has gained a certain amount of notoriety for its 'jobless' nature: increased production has been almost entirely decoupled from employment. Some firms are even downsizing as their profits climb. 'All things being equal, we'd be better off spreading around the work,' observes labour economist Ronald G. Ehrenberg of Cornell University.

Yet a host of factors pushes employers to hire fewer workers for more hours and, at the same time, compels workers to spend more time on the job. Most of those incentives involve what Ehrenberg calls the structure of compensation: quirks in the way salaries and benefits are organised that make it more profitable to ask 40 employees to labour an extra hour each than to hire one more worker to do the same 40-hour job.

Professional and managerial employees supply the most obvious lesson along these lines. Once people are on salary, their cost to a firm is the same whether they spend 35 hours a week in the office or 70. Diminishing returns may eventually set in as overworked employees lose efficiency or leave for more arable pastures. But in the short run, the employer's incentive is clear.

Even hourly employees receive benefits – such as pension contributions and medical insurance – that are not tied to the number of hours they work. Therefore, it is more profitable for employers to work their existing employees harder.

For all that employees complain about long hours, they, too, have reasons not to trade money for leisure. 'People who work reduced hours pay a huge penalty in career terms,' Schor maintains. 'It's taken as a negative signal' about their commitment to the firm.' [Lotte] Bailyn [of Massachusetts Institute of Technology] adds that many corporate managers find it difficult to measure the contribution of their underlings to a firm's well-being, so they use the number of hours worked as a proxy for output. 'Employees know this,' she says, and they adjust their behavior accordingly.

'Although the image of the good worker is the one whose life belongs to the company,' Bailyn says, 'it doesn't fit the facts.' She cites both quantitative and qualitative studies that show increased productivity for part-time workers: they make better use of the time they have, and they are less likely to succumb to fatigue in stressful jobs. Companies that employ more workers for less time also gain from the resulting redundancy, she asserts. 'The extra people can cover the contingencies

that you know are going to happen, such as when crises take people away from the workplace.' Positive experiences with reduced hours have begun to change the more-is-better culture at some companies, Schor reports.

Larger firms, in particular, appear to be more willing to experiment with flexible working arrangements. ...

It may take even more than changes in the financial and cultural structures of employment for workers successfully to trade increased productivity and money for leisure time, Schor contends. She says the U.S. market for goods has become skewed by the assumption of full-time, two-career households. Automobile makers no longer manufacture cheap models, and developers do not build the tiny bungalows that served the first post-war generation of home buyers. Not even the humblest household object is made without a microprocessor. As Schor notes, the situation is a curious inversion of the 'appropriate technology' vision that designers have had for developing countries: U.S. goods are appropriate only for high incomes and long hours.

Paul Wallich

Questions 27–32

Do the following statements agree with the views of the writer in Reading Passage 3? In boxes 27–32 write

> **YES**   *if the statement agrees with the views of the writer*
> **NO**   *if the statement contradicts the views of the writer*
> **NOT GIVEN** *if it is impossible to say what the writer thinks about this*

Example	*Answer*
During the industrial revolution people worked harder.	NOT GIVEN

27   Today, employees are facing a reduction in working hours.

28   Social planners have been consulted about US employment figures.

29   Salaries have not risen significantly since the 1970s.

30   The economic recovery created more jobs.

31   Bailyn's research shows that part-time employees work more efficiently.

32   Increased leisure time would benefit two-career households.

Questions 33–34

Choose the appropriate letters A–D and write them in boxes 33 and 34 on your answer sheet.

33   Bailyn argues that it is better for a company to employ more workers because

  A   it is easy to make excess staff redundant.
  B   crises occur if you are under-staffed.
  C   people are available to substitute for absent staff.
  D   they can project a positive image at work.

34   Schor thinks it will be difficult for workers in the US to reduce their working hours because

  A   they would not be able to afford cars or homes.
  B   employers are offering high incomes for long hours.
  C   the future is dependent on technological advances.
  D   they do not wish to return to the humble post-war era.

Questions 35–38

*The writer mentions a number of factors that have resulted in employees working longer hours. Which **FOUR** of the following factors are mentioned? Write your answers (**A – H**) in boxes 35–38 on your answer sheet.*

List of Factors

A	Books are available to help employees cope with stress.
B	Extra work is offered to existing employees.
C	Increased production has led to joblessness.
D	Benefits and hours spent on the job are not linked.
E	Overworked employees require longer to do their work.
F	Longer hours indicate greater commitment to the firm.
G	Managers estimate staff productivity in terms of hours worked.
H	Employees value a career more than a family.

WRITING

WRITING TASK 1

You should spend about 20 minutes on this task.

> *The chart below shows the amount of money per week spent on fast foods in Britain. The graph shows the trends in consumption of fast foods.*
>
> *Write a report for a university lecturer describing the information shown below.*

You should write at least 150 words.

Expenditure on fast foods by income groups

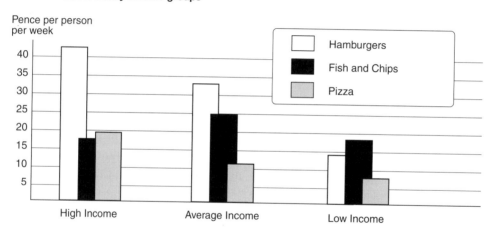

Consumption of fast foods 1970 - 1990

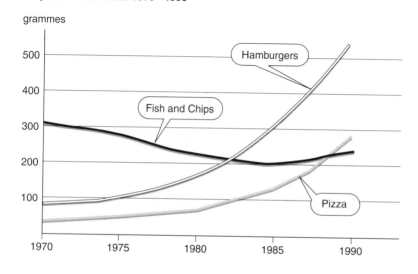

WRITING TASK 2

You should spend about 40 minutes on this task.

Present a written argument or case to an educated reader with no specialist knowledge of the following topic:

> *News editors decide what to broadcast on television and what to print in newspapers. What factors do you think influence these decisions? Do we become used to bad news? Would it be better if more good news was reported?*

You should write at least 250 words.

Use your own ideas, knowledge and experience and support your arguments with examples and relevant evidence.

SPEAKING

CANDIDATE'S CUE CARD   **Task 3**

THE PUBLIC HOLIDAY

There will soon be a public holiday in the country your examiner comes from. You want to find out about the holiday.

Ask the examiner about: the name of the public holiday
the significance of the holiday
availability of services on the day
  (banks/shops/cinemas)
things for visitors to do
how she/he plans to spend the day

INTERVIEWER'S NOTES

THE PUBLIC HOLIDAY

Choose a lesser known public holiday from your country. Be prepared to provide some accurate information on the history and significance of the day. If in-country, tell the candidate how you will spend the day.

If you are in a non-English speaking country, tell the candidate how people normally spend this day back home.

Provide information about the availability of shops, services and banks on the day.

Note: A revised Speaking Module will be operational from July 2001. See page 155 for details and sample tasks.

Practice Test 4

SECTION 1   *Questions 1–12*

Questions 1–5

Circle the appropriate letter.

Example	**What are the students looking for?**		
Ⓐ	Main Hall	**C**	Old Hall
B	Great Hall	**D**	Old Building

1   Where is the administration building?

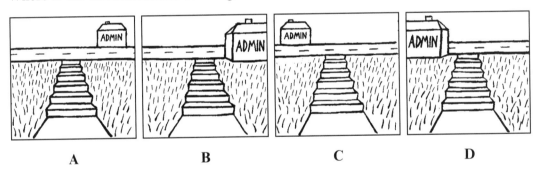

       A   **B**   **C**   **D**

2   How many people are waiting in the queue?

       A 50   **B** 100   **C** 200   **D** 300

3   What does the woman order for lunch?

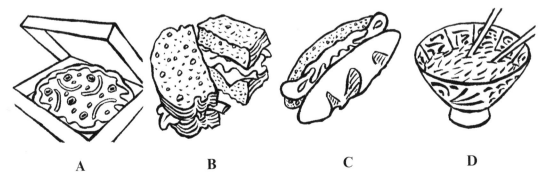

       A   **B**   **C**   **D**

4   What does the woman order to drink?

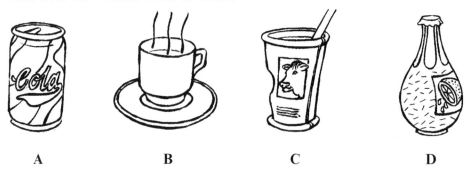

A   B   C   D

5   How much money does the woman give the man?

       A $2.00   **B** $3.00   **C** $3.50   **D** $5.00

Questions 6–10

Complete the registration form using **NO MORE THAN THREE WORDS***.*

Name of student:	**(6)**	....
Address:	**(7)** Flat 5/	....
Town:	**(8)**	....
Tel:	**(9)**	....
Course:	**(10)**	....

Questions 11–12

11   What did the man buy for her to eat?

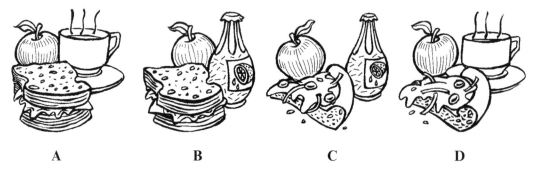

A   B   C   D

12   What must the students do as part of registration at the university?

     A   Check the notice board in the Law Faculty.
     B   Find out about lectures.
     C   Organise tutorial groups.
     D   Pay the union fees.

SECTION 2   *Questions 13–21*

*Complete the notes. Write **NO MORE THAN THREE WORDS** for each answer.*

STUDENT BANKING

Recommended Banks	Location
Barclays	Realty Square
National Westminster	Example: *Preston Park*
Lloyds	City Plaza
Midland	**(13)** ....

Note: May not be allowed all facilities given to resident students.

Funding

■ Must provide **(14)** .... I can support myself.

■ Services will depend on personal circumstances and discretion of Bank Manager.

Opening an account

■ Take with me: **(15)** .... and letter of enrolment.

■ Recommended account: **(16)** ....

■ Bank supplies: **(17)** .... and chequecard which guarantees cheques.

Other services

■ Cashcard: (you can **(18)** .... cash at any time.)

■ Switch/Delta cards: (take the money **(19)** .... the account.)

Overdraft

■ Must have **(20)** ....

■ Sometimes must pay interest.

Opening times

■ Most banks open until **(21)** .... during the week.

■ Some open for a limited time on Saturdays.

SECTION 3   *Questions 22–31*

Questions 22–25

*Complete the factsheet. Write **NO MORE THAN THREE WORDS** for each answer.*

FACTSHEET – Aluminium Cans

- **(22)** .... produced every day in the US – more cans produced than nails or **(23)** ....

- each can weighs 0.48 ounces – thinner than two **(24)** ....

- can take more than 90 pounds of pressure per square inch – over **(25)** .... the pressure of a car tyre

---

Questions 26–31

*Label the aluminium can. Write **NO MORE THAN THREE WORDS** for each answer.*

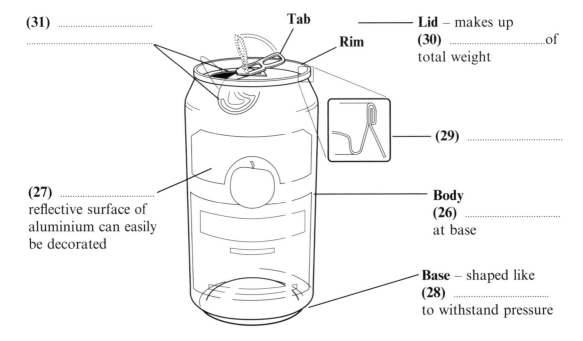

(31) ....
....

Tab

Rim

Lid – makes up **(30)** ....of total weight

(29) ....

(27) ....
reflective surface of
aluminium can easily
be decorated

Body
(26) ....
at base

Base – shaped like **(28)** ....
to withstand pressure

SECTION 4   *Questions 32–42*

Questions 32–42

Complete the lecture notes. Use **NO MORE THAN THREE WORDS** *for each answer.*

Purpose of the mini lecture	
To experience	To find out about
(32)	(33) ....

The three strands of Sports Studies are:
a   **Sports psychology**
b   **Sports (34)** ....
c   **Sports physiology**

a	The psychologists work with	(35) ....
	They want to discover what	(36) ....
b	Sports marketing looks at	(37) ....
	Sport now competes with	(38) ....
	Spectators want	(39) ....
c	Sports physiology is also known as	
		(40) ....
	Macro levels look at	(41) ....
	Micro level looks at	(42) ....

READING

READING PASSAGE 1

*You should spend about 20 minutes on **Questions 1–13** which are based on Reading Passage 1 below.*

GLASS

CAPTURING THE DANCE OF LIGHT

A Glass, in one form or another, has long been in noble service to humans. As one of the most widely used of manufactured materials, and certainly the most versatile, it can be as imposing as a telescope mirror the width of a tennis court or as small and simple as a marble rolling across dirt. The uses of this adaptable material have been broadened dramatically by new technologies: glass fibre optics – more than eight million miles – carrying telephone and television signals across nations; glass ceramics serving as the nose cones of missiles and as crowns for teeth; tiny glass beads taking radiation doses inside the body to specific organs; even a new type of glass fashioned of nuclear waste in order to dispose of that unwanted material.

B On the horizon are optical computers. These could store programs and process information by means of light – pulses from tiny lasers – rather than electrons. And the pulses would travel over glass fibres, not copper wire. These machines could function hundreds of times faster than today's electronic computers and hold vastly more information. Today fibre optics are used to obtain a clearer image of smaller and

smaller objects than ever before – even bacterial viruses. A new generation of optical instruments is emerging that can provide detailed imaging of the inner workings of cells. It is the surge in fibre optic use and in liquid crystal displays that has set the U.S. glass industry (a 16 billion dollar business employing some 150,000 workers) to building new plants to meet demand.

C But it is not only in technology and commerce that glass has widened its horizons. The use of glass as art, a tradition going back at least to Roman times, is also booming. Nearly everywhere, it seems, men and women are blowing glass and creating works of art. 'I didn't sell a piece of glass until 1975,' Dale Chihuly said, smiling, for in the 18 years since the end of the dry spell, he has become one of the most financially successful artists of the 20th century. He now has a new commission – a glass sculpture for the headquarters building of a pizza company – for which his fee is half a million dollars.

D But not all the glass technology that touches our lives is ultra-modern. Consider the simple light bulb; at the turn of the century most light bulbs were hand blown, and the cost of one was equivalent to half a day's pay for the average worker. In effect, the invention of the ribbon machine by Corning in the 1920s lighted a nation. The price of a bulb plunged. Small wonder that the machine has been called one of the great mechanical achievements of all time. Yet it is very simple: a narrow ribbon of molten glass travels over a moving belt of steel in which there are holes. The glass sags through the holes and into waiting moulds. Puffs of

compressed air then shape the glass. In this way, the envelope of a light bulb is made by a single machine at the rate of 66,000 an hour, as compared with 1,200 a day produced by a team of four glassblowers.

E The secret of the versatility of glass lies in its interior structure. Although it is rigid, and thus like a solid, the atoms are arranged in a random disordered fashion, characteristic of a liquid. In the melting process, the atoms in the raw materials are disturbed from their normal position in the molecular structure; before they can find their way back to crystalline arrangements the glass cools. This looseness in molecular structure gives the material what engineers call tremendous 'formability' which allows technicians to tailor glass to whatever they need.

F Today, scientists continue to experiment with new glass mixtures and building designers test their imaginations with applications of special types of glass. A London architect, Mike Davies, sees even more dramatic buildings using molecular chemistry. 'Glass is the great building material of the future, the "dynamic skin",' he said. 'Think of glass that has been treated to react to electric currents going through it, glass that will change from clear to opaque at the push of a button, that gives you instant curtains. Think of how the tall buildings in New York could perform a symphony of colours as the glass in them is made to change colours instantly.' Glass as instant curtains is available now, but the cost is exorbitant. As for the glass changing colours instantly, that may come true. Mike Davies's vision may indeed be on the way to fulfilment.

Adapted from 'Glass: Capturing the Dance of Light' by William S. Ellis, National Geographic

Questions 1–5

Reading Passage 1 has six paragraphs (A–F). Choose the most suitable heading for each paragraph from the list of headings below. Write the appropriate numbers (i–x) in boxes 1–5 on your answer sheet. Paragraph A has been done for you as an example.

NB   There are more headings than paragraphs so you will not use all of them.
You may use any heading more than once.

Example	*Answer*
Paragraph A	**x**

List of Headings

i	Growth in the market for glass crafts
ii	Computers and their dependence on glass
iii	What makes glass so adaptable
iv	Historical development of glass
v	Scientists' dreams cost millions
vi	Architectural experiments with glass
vii	Glass art galleries flourish
viii	Exciting innovations in fibre optics
ix	A former glass technology
x	Everyday uses of glass

1   Paragraph B

2   Paragraph C

3   Paragraph D

4   Paragraph E

5   Paragraph F

Questions 6–8

*The diagram below shows the principle of Corning's ribbon machine. Label the diagram by selecting **NO MORE THAN THREE WORDS** from the Reading Passage to fill each numbered space. Write your answers in boxes 6–8 on your answer sheet.*

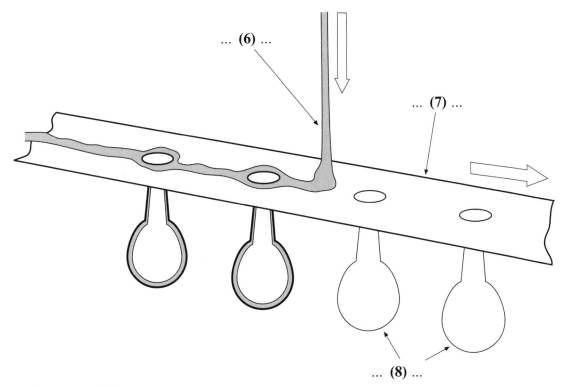

... **(6)** ...

... **(7)** ...

... **(8)** ...

Questions 9–13

Look at the list below of the uses of glass. According to the passage, state whether these uses exist today, will exist in the future or are not mentioned by the writer. In boxes 9–13 write

A   *if the uses exist today*
B   *if the uses will exist in the future*
C   *if the uses are not mentioned by the writer*

9   dental fittings

10   optical computers

11   sculptures

12   fashions

13   curtains

READING PASSAGE 2

*You should spend about 20 minutes on **Questions 14–27** which are based on Reading Passage 2 below.*

Why some women cross the finish line ahead of men

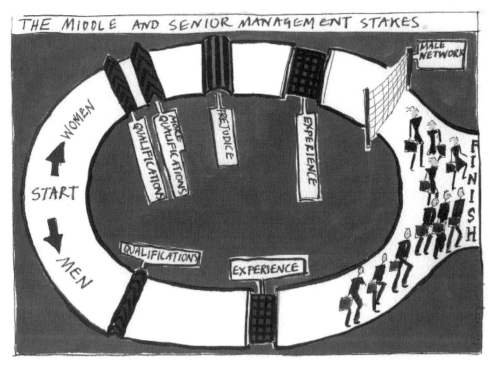

RECRUITMENT

The course is tougher but women are staying the distance, reports **Andrew Crisp.**

A Women who apply for jobs in middle or senior management have a higher success rate than men, according to an employment survey. But of course far fewer of them apply for these positions. The study, by recruitment consultants NB Selection, shows that while one in six men who appear on interview shortlists get jobs, the figure rises to one in four for women.

B The study concentrated on applications for management positions in the $45,000 to $110,000 salary range and found that women are more successful than men in both the private and public sectors. Dr Elisabeth Marx from London-based NB Selection described the findings as encouraging for women, in that they send a positive message to them to apply for interesting management positions. But she added, 'We should not lose sight of the fact that significantly fewer women apply for senior positions in comparison with men.'

C Reasons for higher success rates among women are difficult to isolate. One explanation suggested is that if a woman candidate manages to get on a shortlist, then she has probably already proved herself to be an exceptional candidate. Dr Marx said that when women apply for positions they tend to be better qualified than their male counterparts but are more selective and conservative in their job search. Women tend to research thoroughly before applying for positions or attending interviews. Men, on the other hand, seem to rely on their ability to sell themselves and to convince employers that any shortcomings they have will not prevent them from doing a good job.

D Managerial and executive progress made by women is confirmed by the annual survey of boards of directors carried out by Korn/Ferry/Carre/ Orban International. This year the survey shows a doubling of the number of women serving as non-executive directors compared with the previous year. However, progress remains painfully slow and there were still only 18 posts filled by women out of a total of 354 non-executive positions surveyed. Hilary Sears, a partner with Korn/Ferry, said, 'Women have raised the level of grades we are employed in but we have still not broken through barriers to the top.'

E In Europe a recent feature of corporate life in the recession has been the de-layering of management structures. Sears said that this has halted progress for women in as much as de-layering has taken place either where women are working or in layers they aspire to. Sears also noted a positive trend from the recession, which has been the growing number of women who have started up on their own.

F In business as a whole, there are a number of factors encouraging the prospect of greater equality in the workforce. Demographic trends suggest that the number of women going into employment is steadily increasing. In addition a far greater number of women are now passing through higher education, making them better qualified to move into management positions.

G Organisations such as the European Women's Management Development Network provide a range of opportunities for women to enhance their skills and contacts. Through a series of both pan-European and national workshops and conferences the barriers to women in employment are being broken down. However, Ariane Berthoin Antal, director of the International Institute for Organisational Change of Archamps in France, said that there is only anecdotal evidence of changes in recruitment patterns. And she said, 'It's still so hard for women to even get on to shortlists – there are so many hurdles and barriers.' Antal agreed that there have been some positive signs but said 'Until there is a belief among employers, until they value the difference, nothing will change.'

Questions 14–19

*Reading Passage 2 has 7 paragraphs (**A–G**). State which paragraph discusses each of the points below. Write the appropriate letter (**A–G**) in boxes 14–19 on your answer sheet.*

Example	*Answer*
The salary range studied in the NB Selection survey.	**B**

14 The drawbacks of current company restructuring patterns.

15 Associations that provide support for professional women.

16 The success rate of female job applicants for management positions.

17 Male and female approaches to job applications.

18 Reasons why more women are being employed in the business sector.

19 The improvement in female numbers on company management structures.

Questions 20–23

The author makes reference to three consultants in the Reading Passage. Which of the list of points below do these consultants make? In boxes 20–23 write

> **M** *if the point is made by Dr Marx*
> **S** *if the point is made by Hilary Sears*
> **A** *if the point is made by Ariane Berthoin Antal*

20 Selection procedures do not favour women.

21 The number of female-run businesses is increasing.

22 Male applicants exceed female applicants for top posts.

23 Women hold higher positions now than they used to.

Questions 24–27

*Using **NO MORE THAN THREE WORDS** answer the following questions. Write your answers in boxes 24–27 on your answer sheet.*

24 What change has there been in the number of women in top management positions detailed in the annual survey?

25 What aspect of company structuring has disadvantaged women?

26 What information tells us that more women are working nowadays?

27 Which group of people should change their attitude to recruitment?

READING PASSAGE 3

*You should spend about 20 minutes on **Questions 28–39** which are based on Reading Passage 3 below.*

Population viability analysis

Part A

To make political decisions about the extent and type of forestry in a region it is important to understand the consequences of those decisions. One tool for assessing the impact of forestry on the ecosystem is population viability analysis (PVA). This is a tool for predicting the probability that a species will become extinct in a particular region over a specific period. It has been successfully used in the United States to provide input into resource exploitation decisions and assist wildlife managers and there is now enormous potential for using population viability to assist wildlife management in Australia's forests.

A species becomes extinct when the last individual dies. This observation is a useful starting point for any discussion of extinction as it highlights the role of luck and chance in the extinction process. To make a prediction about extinction we need to understand the processes that can contribute to it and these fall into four broad categories which are discussed below.

Part B

A Early attempts to predict population viability were based on demographic uncertainty. Whether an individual survives from one year to the next will largely be a matter of chance. Some pairs may produce several young in a single year while others may produce none in that same year. Small populations will fluctuate enormously because of the random nature of birth and death and these chance fluctuations can cause species extinctions even if, on average, the population size should increase. Taking only this uncertainty of ability to reproduce into account, extinction is unlikely if the number of individuals in a population is above about 50 and the population is growing.

B Small populations cannot avoid a certain amount of inbreeding. This is particularly true if there is a very small number of one sex. For example, if there are only 20 individuals of a species and only one is a male, all future individuals in the species must be descended from that one male. For most animal species such individuals are less likely to survive and reproduce. Inbreeding increases the chance of extinction.

C Variation within a species is the raw material upon which natural selection acts. Without genetic variability a species lacks the capacity to evolve and cannot adapt to changes in its environment or to new predators and new diseases. The loss of genetic diversity associated with reductions in population size will contribute to the likelihood of extinction.

D Recent research has shown that other factors need to be considered. Australia's environment fluctuates enormously from year to year. These fluctuations add yet another degree of uncertainty to the survival of many species. Catastrophes such as fire, flood, drought or epidemic may reduce population sizes to a small fraction of their average level. When allowance is made for these two additional elements of uncertainty the population size necessary to be confident of persistence for a few hundred years may increase to several thousand.

Part C

Beside these processes we need to bear in mind the distribution of a population. A species that occurs in five isolated places each containing 20 individuals will not have the same probability of extinction as a species with a single population of 100 individuals in a single locality.

Where logging occurs (that is, the cutting down of forests for timber) forest-dependent creatures in that area will be forced to leave. Ground-dwelling herbivores may return within a decade. However, arboreal marsupials (that is animals which live in trees) may not recover to pre-logging densities for over a century. As more forests are logged, animal population sizes will be reduced further. Regardless of the theory or model that we choose, a reduction in population size decreases the genetic diversity of a population and increases the probability of extinction because of any or all of the processes listed above. It is therefore a scientific fact that increasing the area that is logged in any region will increase the probability that forest-dependent animals will become extinct.

Questions 28–31

Do the following statements agree with the views of the writer in Part A of Reading Passage 3? In boxes 28–31 on your answer sheet write

YES   *if the statement agrees with the writer*
NO   *if the statement contradicts the writer*
NOT GIVEN   *if it is impossible to say what the writer thinks about this*

Example	*Answer*
A link exists between the consequences of decisions and the decision making process itself.	**YES**

28   Scientists are interested in the effect of forestry on native animals.

29   PVA has been used in Australia for many years.

30   A species is said to be extinct when only one individual exists.

31   Extinction is a naturally occurring phenomenon.

Questions 32–35

These questions are based on Part B of Reading Passage 3.

In paragraphs A to D the author describes four processes which may contribute to the extinction of a species. Match the list of processes (i–vi) to the paragraphs. Write the appropriate number (i–vi) in boxes 32–35 on your answer sheet.

NB   There are more processes than paragraphs so you will not use all of them.

		Processes	
32	Paragraph A	**i**	Loss of ability to adapt
33	Paragraph B	**ii**	Natural disasters
		iii	An imbalance of the sexes
34	Paragraph C	**iv**	Human disasters
35	Paragraph D	**v**	Evolution
		vi	The haphazard nature of reproduction

Questions 36–38

*Based on your reading of Part C, complete the sentences below with words taken from the passage. Use **NO MORE THAN THREE WORDS** for each answer. Write your answers in boxes 36–38 on your answer sheet.*

While the population of a species may be on the increase, there is always a chance that small isolated groups ... **(36)** ...

Survival of a species depends on a balance between the size of a population and its ... **(37)** ...

The likelihood that animals which live in forests will become extinct is increased when ... **(38)** ...

Question 39

Choose the appropriate letter A–D and write it in box 39 on your answer sheet.

39   An alternative heading for the passage could be:

    A   The protection of native flora and fauna
    B   Influential factors in assessing survival probability
    C   An economic rationale for the logging of forests
    D   Preventive measures for the extinction of a species

WRITING

WRITING TASK 1

You should spend about 20 minutes on this task.

> *Chorleywood is a village near London whose population has increased steadily since the middle of the nineteenth century. The map below shows the development of the village.*
>
> *Write a report for a university lecturer describing the development of the village.*

You should write at least 150 words.

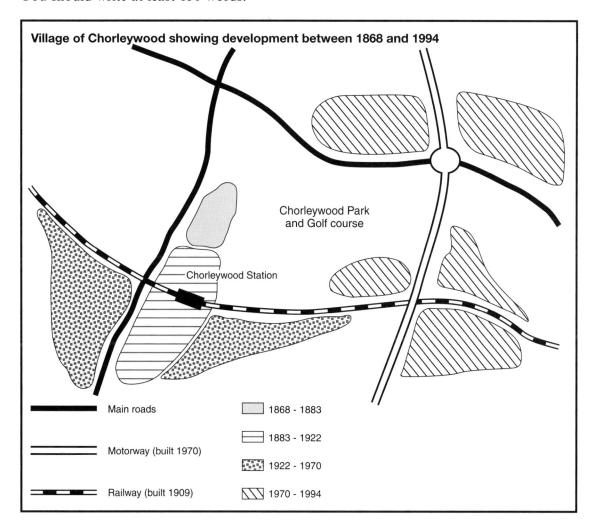

Village of Chorleywood showing development between 1868 and 1994

Main roads

Motorway (built 1970)

Railway (built 1909)

Chorleywood Park and Golf course

Chorleywood Station

1868 - 1883

1883 - 1922

1922 - 1970

1970 - 1994

WRITING TASK 2

You should spend about 40 minutes on this task.

Present a written argument or case to an educated reader with no specialist knowledge of the following topic:

> *The idea of having a single career is becoming an old fashioned one. The new fashion will be to have several careers or ways of earning money and further education will be something that continues throughout life.*

You should write at least 250 words.

Use your own ideas, knowledge and experience and support your arguments with examples and relevant evidence.

SPEAKING

CANDIDATE'S CUE CARD   **Task 4**

THE EXCURSION

The Overseas Students' Club is organising an excursion to a local tourist spot. You are thinking of joining the excursion. Your examiner is one of the organisers.

Ask the examiner about: destination
                                        means of transport
                                        length of excursion
                                        cost
                                        meals
                                        clothing/equipment

INTERVIEWER'S NOTES

THE EXCURSION

Select an authentic tourist destination about two hours' drive from your city. Provide the following information according to local facts:

- Details about what can be seen/done there

- Special bus provided

- Departure and arrival times

- Suggest appropriate local cost

- Meals not provided – students can buy or bring food

- Walking shoes recommended

Note: A revised Speaking Module will be operational from July 2001. See page 155 for details and sample tasks.

General Training Module

PART ONE

*You are advised to spend 20 minutes on **Questions 1–14**. First, read the text below and answer **Questions 1–8**.*

YOUR MOULEX IRON

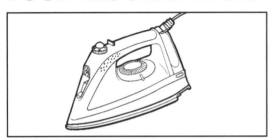

A   Filling the reservoir

Your iron is designed to function using tap water. However, it will last longer if you use distilled water.
– Always unplug the iron before filling the reservoir.
– Always empty the reservoir after use.

B   Temperature and steam control

Your Moulex iron has two buttons which control the intensity of heat produced by the iron. You can, therefore, adjust the temperature of the iron and the amount of steam being given off depending upon the type of fabric being ironed.
– Turn the steam control to the desired intensity.
– Turn the thermostat control to the desired temperature.
Important: *If your iron produces droplets of water instead of giving off steam, your temperature control is set too low.*

C   Spray button

This button activates a jet of cold water which allows you to iron out any unintentional creases. Press the button for one second.

D   Pressing button

This button activates a super shot of steam which momentarily gives you an additional 40g of steam, when needed.
Important: *Do not use this more than five successive times.*

E   Suits etc.

It is possible to use this iron in a vertical position so that you can remove creases from clothes on coathangers or from curtains. Turning the thermostat control and the steam button to maximum, hold the iron in a vertical position close to the fabric but without touching it. Hold down the pressing button for a maximum of one second. The steam produced is not always visible but is still able to remove creases.
Important: *Hold the iron at a sufficient distance from silk and wool to avoid all risk of scorching. Do not attempt to remove creases from an item of clothing that is being worn, always use a coathanger.*

F   Auto-clean

In order that your iron does not become furred up, Moulex have integrated an auto-clean system and we advise you to use it very regularly (1–2 times per month).
– Turn the steam control to the off position.
– Fill the reservoir and turn the thermostat control to maximum.
– As soon as the indicator light goes out, unplug the iron and, holding it over the sink, turn the steam control to auto-clean. Any calcium deposits will be washed out by the steam. Continue the procedure until the reservoir is empty.

Questions 1–4

*Match the pictures below to the appropriate section in the instructions. Write the correct letter **A–F** in boxes 1–4 on your answer sheet.*

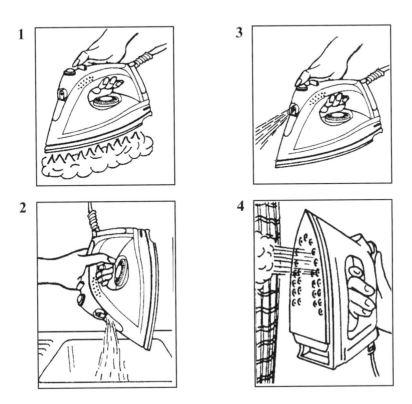

Questions 5–8

*Answer the following questions on the Moulex iron using **NO MORE THAN THREE WORDS**. Write your answers in boxes 5–8 on your answer sheet.*

5   What sort of water are you advised to use?

6   What factor makes you decide on the quantity of steam to use?

7   What should you do if your iron starts to drip water?

8   What could damage your iron if you do not clean it?

*Now, read the information below and answer **Questions 9–14**.*

CLASSIC TOURS – COACH BREAK INFORMATION

Luggage
We ask you to keep luggage down to one medium-sized suitcase per person, but a small holdall can also be taken on board the coach.

Seat Allocation
Requests for particular seats can be made on most coach breaks when booking, but since allocations are made on a first come first served basis, early booking is advisable. When bookings are made with us you will be offered the best seats that are available on the coach at that time.

Travel Documents
When you have paid your deposit we will send to you all the necessary documents and labels, so that you receive them in good time before the coach break departure date. Certain documents, for example air or boat tickets, may have to be retained and your driver or courier will then issue them to you at the relevant point.

Special Diets
If you require a special diet you must inform us at the time of booking with a copy of the diet. This will be notified to the hotel or hotels on your coach break, but on certain coach breaks the hotels used are tourist class and whilst offering value for money within the price range, they may not have the full facilities to cope with special diets. Any extra costs incurred must be paid to the hotel by yourself before departure from the hotel.

Accommodation
Many of our coach breaks now include, within the price, accommodation with private facilities, and this will be indicated on the coach break page. Other coach breaks have a limited number of rooms with private facilities which, subject to availability, can be reserved and guaranteed at the time of booking – the supplementary charge shown in the price panel will be added to your account.

On any coach break there are only a limited number of single rooms. When a single room is available it may be subject to a supplementary charge and this will be shown on the brochure page.

Entertainment
Some of our hotels arrange additional entertainment which could include music, dancing, film shows, etc. The nature and frequency of the entertainment presented is at the discretion of the hotel and therefore not guaranteed and could be withdrawn if there is a lack of demand or insufficient numbers in the hotel.

Questions 9–14

*Choose the appropriate letters **A–D** and write them in boxes 9–14 on your answer sheet.*

9 If you want to sit at the front of the coach

    A   ask when you get on the coach.
    B   arrive early on the departure date.
    C   book your seat well in advance.
    D   avoid travelling at peak times.

10 Your air tickets

    A   will be sent to your departure point.
    B   must be collected before leaving.
    C   will be enclosed with other documents.
    D   may be held by your coach driver.

11 If you need a special diet you should

    A   inform the hotel when you arrive.
    B   pay extra with the booking.
    C   tell the coach company.
    D   book tourist class.

12 It may be necessary to pay extra for

    A   a bathroom.
    B   boat tickets.
    C   additional luggage.
    D   entertainment.

13 Entertainment is available

    A   at all hotels.
    B   if there is the demand.
    C   upon request.
    D   for an additional cost.

14 With every booking Classic Tours guarantee you will be able to

    A   request high quality meals.
    B   take hand luggage on the coach.
    C   use your own personal bathroom.
    D   see a film if you want to.

PART TWO

You are advised to spend 20 minutes on Questions 15–29.

Questions 15–21

Look at the article Clubs for Students. *Which club would you contact for each of the requirements below? Write the appropriate letter **A–G** in boxes 15–21 on your answer sheet. You may use each letter more than once.*
The first one has been done for you as an example.

Example	*Answer*
You wish to go swimming at 7am every morning.	**G**

15 You would like to take Spanish classes.

16 You want to join a club that has international branches.

17 You would like an opportunity to speak in public.

18 You would like to take part in amateur theatrical productions.

19 You want to visit some famous sites with a group of other students.

20 You are interested in finding out about part-time work.

21 You want to meet some English people who have started their careers.

CLUBS FOR STUDENTS

There are a variety of Clubs which provide social and cultural activities for those wishing to meet others with similar interests from the same or from different national backgrounds.

A Commonwealth Trust

Organised discussion meetings, learned talks, cultural events, excursions to places of interest and invitations to major British diary events. Open to overseas visitors and students.

B Charles Péguy Centre

French youth centre providing advice, support and information to young Europeans aged between 18–30. Facilities include an information and advice service regarding education, work placement and general welfare rights. Moreover the centre holds a database of jobs, accommodation and au pair placements, specifically in London. Members may use a fax machine, a copier and computers for CVs.
Hours: Monday: 14.00–17.00
             Tuesday–Friday: 10.00–17.00
Membership: £35 per year, plus £5 per month.

C Kensington Committee of Friendship for Overseas Students

KCOF is the society for young people from all countries. Each month there are some 40 parties, discos, visits to theatres, concerts,walks and other gatherings where you will be able to meet lots of people. A new programme is sent each month directly to members (£5 to join in October, less later in the year). Events are free or at low, often reduced, prices. Office open 10.30–17.30 weekdays only.

D Royal Overseas League

Open 365 days per year, this is a club with facilities in London and Edinburgh with restaurants, bars and accommodation. There are branches around the world and 57 reciprocal clubs world-wide. Quarterly magazine, literary lectures, annual music and art competitions, and summer and winter programme of events for members. Membership fees: overseas students aged 17–24 £47 per year + initial joining fee £23.50; others £70 per year + initial joining fee £35 (half price after July). Further information from the Membership Secretary.

E YMCA London Central

Facilities include: photography, art, drama, pottery, language courses, badminton, squash, exercise to music, circuit training, sports clinic, fitness testing and other activities.
Hours: weekdays 07.00–22.30, weekends 10.00–21.00. Membership fees: aged 16–17 £25 per year plus attendance charge of £1.30 per visit; aged 18–19 £213 per year; aged 20–25 £366 per year.

F London Inter-Varsity Club (IVC)

IVC is an activities and social club with a varied range of events, from cycling and drama to windsurfing and yoga. Most members are young English professionals, but overseas visitors are welcome. The club arranges restaurant meals, dancing and parties, weekends away around Britain, plus a weekly club night in a Covent Garden bar. There are usually over 25 different events every week run by IVC members for IVC members. To find out more, telephone the club or write (Freepost) to the office.

G Central Club

Provides accommodation and club facilities. No membership fee. Coffee shop open for all meals, swimming pool (open 06.00), multi-gym, hairdressing salon.

Questions 22–29

Read the article on International Students House and look at the statements below.
In boxes 22–29 on your answer sheet write

TRUE	*if the statement is true*
FALSE	*if the statement is false*
NOT GIVEN	*if the information is not given in the passage*

The first one has been done for you as an example.

Example	*Answer*
The club is for overseas students only.	**FALSE**

22   The club has long-term dormitory accommodation.

23   Membership must be renewed monthly.

24   The club provides subsidised restaurant meals.

25   The club is open to non-members on Tuesday evenings.

26   STA Travel help finance the Students Adviser.

27   The services of the Students Adviser are free to all club members.

28   You must make an appointment to see the Students Adviser.

29   There will be a surcharge for accommodation over the Christmas period.

INTERNATIONAL STUDENTS HOUSE

International Students House is a unique club and accommodation centre for British and overseas students in London. It is located in the heart of London's West End and is close to all public transport facilities.

ACCOMMODATION
★ comfortable accommodation for up to 450 people in single, twin, 3/4 bedded and multi-bedded rooms
★ 44 self-contained flats for married students and families
★ long and short stays welcomed

MEMBERSHIP
Club membership is open to all full-time students, professional trainees, student nurses and au pairs. Membership costs are kept to an absolute minimum to enable the widest possible access. You can join for as little as one month and for up to one year at a time. Membership entitles you to use the various facilities of the House. It has:
★ restaurants
★ student bars and coffee shop
★ study rooms
★ clubs and societies
★ aerobics and fitness training
★ discos, dance, jazz and cinema
★ travel and excursions and much more!
The best way to check out all we have on offer is to drop in any Tuesday evening

between 7.15 pm and 8.30 pm for **Open House** in the Club Room. This is an opportunity for you to meet the staff and other club members, enjoy a free cup of coffee and find out all about what's going on. You can take advantage of special membership offers. (Useful tip: bring along 3 passport size photographs if you wish to take out membership.)

ADVICE SERVICE
Thanks to the support of STA Travel and in association with LCOS (the London Conference on Overseas Students) International Students House now provides the service of an International Students Adviser. This new welfare service is open to **all students** at London's bona-fide academic institutions. It aims to provide welfare support to help students overcome any personal or practical difficulties they may be experiencing whilst studying in Britain. One of the key features of the Advice Service is that the Adviser can be seen during the evenings until about 8 pm, Monday to Thursday.

CHRISTMAS & NEW YEAR
Unable to get home for Christmas? How about joining in the fun at International Students House! Check out our special programme of activity taking place over the Christmas period. Even come and stay – the House will be offering reduced accommodation rates for students wishing to spend a few days in London over Christmas. We'll also have an exciting New Year's Eve party so come and join us and ring in the new year in the spirit of internationalism.

PART THREE

READING PASSAGE 3

*You should spend about 20 minutes on **Questions 30–41** which are based on the Reading Passage below.*

PAPER RECYCLING

A Paper is different from other waste produce because it comes from a sustainable resource: trees. Unlike the minerals and oil used to make plastics and metals, trees are replaceable. Paper is also biodegradable, so it does not pose as much threat to the environment when it is discarded. While 45 out of every 100 tonnes of wood fibre used to make paper in Australia comes from waste paper, the rest comes directly from virgin fibre from forests and plantations. By world standards this is a good performance since the world-wide average is 33 per cent waste paper. Governments have encouraged waste paper collection and sorting schemes and at the same time, the paper industry has responded by developing new recycling technologies that have paved the way for even greater utilisation of used fibre. As a result, industry's use of recycled fibres is expected to increase at twice the rate of virgin fibre over the coming years.

B Already, waste paper constitutes 70% of paper used for packaging and advances in the technology required to remove ink from the paper have allowed a higher recycled content in newsprint and writing paper. To achieve the benefits of recycling, the community must also contribute. We need to accept a change in the quality of paper products; for example stationery may be less white and of a rougher texture. There also needs to be support from the community for waste paper collection programs. Not only do we need to make the paper available to collectors but it also needs to be separated into different types and sorted from contaminants such as staples, paperclips, string and other miscellaneous items.

C There are technical limitations to the amount of paper which can be recycled and some paper products cannot be collected for re-use. These include paper in the form of books and permanent records, photographic paper and paper which is badly contaminated. The four most common sources of paper for recycling are factories and retail stores which gather large amounts of packaging material in which goods are delivered, also offices which have unwanted business documents and computer output, paper converters and printers and lastly households which discard newspapers and packaging material. The paper manufacturer pays a price for the paper and may also incur the collection cost.

D Once collected, the paper has to be sorted by hand by people trained to recognise various types of paper. This is necessary because some types of paper can only be made from particular kinds of recycled fibre. The sorted paper then has to be repulped or mixed with water and broken down into its individual fibres. This mixture is called *stock* and may contain a wide variety of contaminating materials, particularly if it is made from mixed waste paper which has had little sorting. Various machinery is used to remove other materials from the stock. After passing through the repulping process, the fibres from printed waste paper are grey in colour because the printing ink has soaked into the individual fibres. This recycled material can only be used in products where the grey colour does not matter, such as cardboard boxes but if the grey colour is not acceptable, the fibres must be de-inked. This involves adding chemicals such as caustic soda or other alkalis, soaps and detergents, water-hardening agents such as calcium chloride, frothing agents and bleaching agents. Before the recycled fibres can be made into paper they must be refined or treated in such a way that they bond together.

E Most paper products must contain some virgin fibre as well as recycled fibres and unlike glass, paper cannot be recycled indefinitely. Most paper is down-cycled which means that a product made from recycled paper is of an inferior quality to the original paper. Recycling paper is beneficial in that it saves some of the energy, labour and capital that goes into producing virgin pulp. However, recycling requires the use of fossil fuel, a non-renewable energy source, to collect the waste paper from the community and to process it to produce new paper. And the recycling process still creates emissions which require treatment before they can be disposed of safely. Nevertheless, paper recycling is an important economical and environmental practice but one which must be carried out in a rational and viable manner for it to be useful to both industry and the community.

Questions 30–36

Complete the summary below of the first two paragraphs of the Reading Passage. Choose **ONE OR TWO WORDS** *from the Reading Passage for each answer. Write your answers in boxes 30–36 on your answer sheet.*

SUMMARY

Example

From the point of view of recycling, paper has two advantages over minerals and ...oil...

in that firstly it comes from a resource which is ... **(30)** ... and secondly it is less

threatening to our environment when we throw it away because it is ... **(31)** ...

Although Australia's record in the re-use of waste paper is good, it is still necessary to

use a combination of recycled fibre and ... **(32)** ... to make new paper. The paper

industry has contributed positively and people have also been encouraged by ... **(33)** ...

to collect their waste on a regular basis. One major difficulty is the removal of ink

from used paper but ... **(34)** ... are being made in this area. However, we need to learn

to accept paper which is generally of a lower ... **(35)** ... than before and to sort our

waste paper by removing ... **(36)** ... before discarding it for collection.

Questions 37–41

Look at paragraphs C, D, and E and, using the information in the passage, complete the flow chart below. Write your answers in boxes 37–41 on your answer sheet. Use **ONE OR TWO WORDS** *for each answer.*

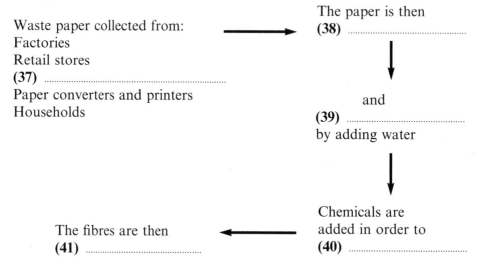

Waste paper collected from:
Factories
Retail stores
(37) ....
Paper converters and printers
Households

→

The paper is then
(38) ....

↓

and
(39) ....
by adding water

↓

Chemicals are
added in order to
(40) ....

←

The fibres are then
(41) ....

WRITING

WRITING TASK 1

You should spend about 20 minutes on this task.

> *You have had a bank account for a few years. Recently you received a letter from the bank stating that your account is $240 overdrawn and that you will be charged $70 which will be taken directly from your account. You know that this information is incorrect.*
>
> *Write a letter to the bank. Explain what has happened and say what you would like them to do about it.*

You should write at least 150 words.

You do **NOT** need to write your own address. Begin your letter as follows:

> *Dear Sir,*

WRITING TASK 2

You should spend about 40 minutes on this task.

As part of a class assignment you have to write about the following topic:

> *We are becoming increasingly dependent on computers. They are used in businesses, hospitals, crime detection and even to fly planes. What things will they be used for in the future? Is this dependence on computers a good thing or should we be more suspicious of their benefits?*

You should write at least 250 words.

Tapescripts

SECTION 1

R = Receptionist
W = Woman
P = Police Officer

R: Good evening, City Police Station. Can I help you?
W: Oh hello, I'd like to report <u>a stolen briefcase,</u> please.   *Example*
R: Just a minute and I'll put you through.
    Repeat
P: Lost property. Can I help you?
W: Oh, yes. I've had my briefcase stolen.
P: OK ... I'll take some details ... Tell me what it looks like, first of all.
W: Well ... it's a <u>soft leather one</u>, you know, not a heavy box-type like a man's.
P: Mmm ... and how does it close?
W: <u>It's got buckles at the front ... two of them.</u> They're gold-plated ones.   *Q1*
P: Fine ... Was it locked?
W: No, I'm afraid not.
P: Never mind. Any distinguishing features?
W: Pardon?
P: Any marks or badges on it that make it stand out?
W: Only the brand name.
P: And where's that?
W: It's on the back ... <u>at the bottom in the left-hand corner. It's Sagi.</u> Oh and   *Q2*
    there's a <u>scratch</u> ... it's quite bad but small ... <u>directly above the brand</u>
    <u>name.</u> I did it recently putting it on my bike.
P: Right, got that. So, what did you have inside the briefcase?
W: Well – <u>all my papers</u> from college. It's so frustrating but, thank goodness for
    computers, I haven't lost them completely!
P: Yes, you're lucky.
W: I had my wallet in my pocket so I didn't lose that but there were also <u>my pens</u>   *Q3*
    which I got for my birthday and <u>a novel</u> I was planning to read on the train.
P: Right. Where exactly did you lose the briefcase?
W: Well ... I couldn't believe it. <u>I was standing on the platform ... it was right</u>
    <u>next to me.</u>
P: You were holding it?
W: <u>I'd just put it down on the floor</u> but I could almost feel it beside me. <u>I was</u>   *Q4*
    <u>watching for my train because sometimes it comes early</u> and then next time I
    looked, my briefcase wasn't there.
P: And what time was this?
W: Ah ... it was ... <u>it must have been about 5.20 ... no a bit later. I'd say 5.30</u>   *Q5*

107

because it was just getting crowded and the train normally comes at about twenty-five to six.

P: Right, if you'll just give me some personal details …
W: Yes.
P: What name is it?
W: I'm Mary Prescott.
P: Can you spell that?
W: Yes, it's P-R-E-S-C-O-T-T.   *Q6*
P: And your address?
W: Flat 2, 41, Fountain Road, Canterbury.   *Qs 7 and 8*
P: Fountain Road.
W: Yes, number 41.
P: And have you got a contact telephone number?
W: Yes, it's 7-5- double 2-3-9.
P: 7-5-double 2-3-9. Fine. One last question – what would you say the value of   *Q9*
    your briefcase is?
W: Including the contents?
P: Yes. Just a rough estimate is fine.
W: I'm not sure. Well, the briefcase itself is quite new; I bought it last month for
    £40. I suppose about £65. The contents are worth about 20 or 25 pounds at   *Q10*
    least.
P: That's fine. Well, if you could come down to the station tomorrow, you can
    sign this form and have a look at what we've got here.
W: OK, thanks. 'Bye.
P: Goodbye.

SECTION 2

Newsreader: This is the 6 o'clock news for Tuesday 25 November. And first the headlines:

The Prime Minister has promised to help the drought stricken farmers in the   *Example*
northern part of the country who haven't seen rain for nearly two years. And in
Sydney a group of school children are successfully rescued from a plane which   *Q11*
landed in the sea shortly after take-off. Transport workers are on strike in
Melbourne over a pay claim and the strike looks set to spread to other states. And *Q12*
on a fashionable note, there's to be a new look for the staff of QANTAS,   *Q13*
Australia's national airline.

The Prime Minister has pledged today that he will make two hundred and fifty   *Q14*
million dollars available to help the drought stricken farmers who have not seen
rain for years, get through the next five years. Money that was to have been spent
on the re-structuring of Sydney's road system has been re-allocated to what the   *Q15*
Prime Minister described as 'a more worthy cause'. Farmers are to receive
financial assistance to help see them through the worst drought in over 50 years.
Many farmers feel that while the money is welcome it has come too late to save   *Q16*

108

them and their farms from financial ruin and are angry that the government did not act sooner.

A group of <u>school children</u> who were travelling in a privately chartered   *Q17*
aeroplane from Sydney to Queensland to take part in a musical concert found
themselves swimming for the shore when their aeroplane had to land in the sea
just <u>three minutes after taking off</u> from Sydney airport. The pilot managed to   *Q18*
bring the aircraft and its 50 passengers down safely in the calm waters of Botany
Bay where <u>boats and pleasurecraft</u> were able to come to the rescue of the boys.   *Q19*
The fact that it was a weekend meant that there were hundreds of boats in
the bay enjoying the good weather and this undoubtedly helped the rescue
operation. '<u>We owe our lives to the skill of the pilot,</u>' said one of the boys, but the   *Q20*
pilot replied modestly that it was 'all part of a day's work'. However, <u>all their</u>   *Q21*
<u>musical instruments were lost</u> and they never got to play at their concert.

SECTION 3

M = male student
F = female lecturer

M: Hello, can I come in?
F: Oh yes, come in. How can I help you?
M: <u>I was looking for the Economics office.</u> I've been all over the Arts Faculty   *Example*
      building looking for it but I could only find the School of Accounting and
      Economic History. Is this the right place?
F: Yes, this is the School of Economics.
M: Oh good. Um, I'm a new student and I was wondering if someone could give
      me some information.
F: Well I might be able to help. I lecture on that program. What do you need to
      know?
M: Quite a few things, actually. Firstly, how many lectures a week do I have to
      attend?
F: Ah, well, the Economics I course is a double unit so there are two lectures a
      week and one tutorial. The lectures are scheduled for Tuesday and Thursday.
M: What time?
F: Let me see … You know this information is all in the <u>handout which you</u>   *Q22*
      <u>should have received yesterday at the orientation meeting.</u>
M: Oh, was there a meeting yesterday? I didn't know about that … no one
      mentioned …
F: Yes, there was, but never mind. Now lectures are at four in the afternoon.
M: Four's a bit late. I've got a part time job that starts at four thirty.
F: Well you can't be in two places at once, can you, and <u>attendance at lectures</u>   *Q23*
      <u>is necessary.</u> We expect at least 90% attendance at this university, you know.
M: 90%! That's high. Do they enforce that rule?
F: Yes, we do. We're pretty strict about it actually.
M: And what times have been set down for the tutorials – do you have that
      information?
F: That's a very well attended course so there's a number of tutorial times.

Monday, Wednesday and Friday, all at 9 o'clock. Yours will be allocated at   *Q24*
the first lecture.

M: Can't I choose the time?

F: Maybe, maybe not. You'll have to talk to the lecturer on the course. Dr   *Q25*
Roberts is his name.

M: Oh, OK.

F: Anything else I can help you with while you're here?

M: Well, yes, actually. Do you know what the course requirements are? I mean,
how much work is expected for this course?

F: Well, you have to complete a tutorial paper.

M: What does that involve?

F: Well, it's a piece of work on a given topic based on some set reading texts.
You'll have to give a small talk to your tutorial group ...   *Q26*

M: How long does that have to be?

F: Oh, about 25 minutes usually.

M: I have to talk for 25 minutes?

F: Yes, that's right. And then you have to write up your piece of work and give   *Q27*
it to the lecturer to be marked.

M: Right. And is that all?

F: No. You also have to complete a 3,000 word essay on a topic.

M: Can I choose the topic?

F: Yes, usually you can.   *Q28*

M: Right. That shouldn't be too bad.

F: And in addition to that there is an exam.

M: An exam! What sort of exam?

F: Well, it's an open book exam.   *Q29*

M: Does that mean I can have the text book with me during the exam?

F: Yes, that's right.

M: And can you give me any idea about the content of the first year of
Economics so that I can get into some reading?

F: Well, you'll be getting the reading list next week when lectures start. All the
books are in the library.

M: Yes, but won't everyone else take them out as soon as they get the reading
list too?

F: Well, yes, they might. But most of the important ones are held in Closed   *Q30*
Reserve ... that's a part of the library where you can go to read books but
you can't take them out of the building.

M: What did you call that section of the library?

F: Closed Reserve. However, we do recommend that you *buy* the core books.
You'll find them useful and you'll need them for the exam.

M: Yes, I suppose I will. But what is the focus of the course?

F: Well, the course at this university has a vocational focus, that is a focus on   *Q31*
preparing its graduates for work, so we're orientated very much towards
employment.

M: So my chances of getting a job are good?

F: Well, provided you get good results.

M: Well look – thanks for your time. You've been really helpful.

F: That's fine. See you next week then.

SECTION 4

Lecturer:

Good morning and welcome to the University of Westlands. My name is Marcia Mayhew and I'm the co-ordinator of the Bachelor of Social Science degree. This morning I'd like to tell you about the structure of the university and about some of the requirements of the degree that you're about to enter. The Bachelor of Social Science is in one faculty within the university; <u>that is the faculty where I</u>   *Q32*
<u>work, known as Arts and Social Sciences</u>. Here on this campus we also have the faculties of Architecture, Law and Science and Technology among others.

   It's important to know something about the structure of the faculty because, as you go through your course, you may need to call on members of the staff to help you.

   At the top of the faculty we have a dean and <u>below the dean we have three</u>   *Q33*
<u>divisions</u>; each division has a divisional head and your degree is located in the Division of Social Sciences. Within each of the divisions, there are the departments and each of these offers the different degrees. For instance, two of the departments which offer the major subjects for your award are Sociology and Psychology. Each has a departmental head but for practical purposes, the people you are going to see the most of are myself as co-ordinator of the social sciences degree and the actual lecturers who are teaching the subjects that you are taking. For instance in the first semester you'll be doing four subjects: psychology, sociology, <u>history and</u>   *Q34*
<u>economics</u>.

   If you have any problems or difficulties, not that I'm anticipating you will, but you never know, then you should go and see your lecturers. For instance, you may find that you <u>can't meet a deadline for an essay</u> or perhaps you're <u>having</u>   *Q35*
<u>problems with attendance</u>. These seem to be the two most common problems that   *Q36*
students face.

   If your lecturers are unavailable, you can always come and see me in *my* office. <u>I'm available on Wednesday and Thursday mornings and on Friday afternoons</u>.   *Q37*
Outside these hours, perhaps you could ring the secretary and make an appointment.

   Now, you'll note that all of the subjects which you undertake in the first year are composed of lectures and tutorials. A lecture is about an hour long and a tutorial usually runs for about two hours. A lecture is rather like what I am doing now, where one person will talk to all of you together on a subject. We do ask you to try to attend the lectures.

   A tutorial is perhaps where most of the learning occurs at a university. You will be divided into groups of between 12 and 15 students and each week one of you will have to present a piece of work to the group as a whole and then the group will discuss what you've said. <u>It's this discussion, this exchange of ideas</u>, which   *Q38*
really constitutes the basis of university learning, in my view. Listening to lectures in many ways is just giving you information that you could access for yourself in

the library, but the discussion at the tutorial is very important. This doesn't mean that you shouldn't go to the lectures though!

Other factors to be particularly concerned about are the structure of essays and delivery of written material and in particular I would like to mention the question of plagiarism. Plagiarism is taking other people's work without acknowledging it, that is, without saying where it comes from. Of course all essays are based on research done by other people <u>but you must remember to attribute the work to the original writer</u>. And while it's a good idea to work with other people, don't hand in work which is exactly the same as your friend's work because we will notice! If you don't acknowledge the source of your information, <u>then you run the risk of failing the subject or in very serious cases you might be denied entry to the university.</u>

Last but not least, stay in touch with us. If things are getting you down, don't go and hide. Come and talk to us about it. That's what we are here for. Right, thank you very much for coming along today.

Q39

Q40

Q41 tests global under-standing of the talk

PRACTICE TEST 2

SECTION 1

C = Counsellor
K = Kate
L = Luki

C: Hi there, Kate. Come on in. How are you today?
K: Fine, thanks.
C: Hi, Luki. How's things?
L: OK.
C: Well, as I explained on the phone, I'm a Counsellor here at the Student Services section of the university and I'm interviewing overseas students to help me draw up a guide for new students so I'd be grateful if you could tell me a little about your time since you've been here in Cambridge.
K: Right.
L: Good idea.
C: Now, Kate, let's start with you. OK, um … this is your second semester, isn't it? Could you tell us something about your first impressions of the town when you arrived?
K: Yeah, well, first of all I was struck by <u>how quiet it is here</u> in the evening. *Repeat*
C: Yes, I suppose Cambridge is a quiet place. Where did you live when you first arrived?
K: Well, I went straight into <u>student accommodation</u>; it was a kind of <u>student hostel</u>.
C: Ah right, so you didn't have to worry about doing your own cooking or anything like that?

Example

Q1

K: No, but sometimes I wished I had! <u>The food at the hostel was awful.</u> Q2

C: Oh dear. But how were the other students?

K: To be honest I haven't managed to make many friends even though the place is full. People seem to keep to themselves; <u>they're not really very friendly.</u> Q3

C: Oh, I'm sorry to hear that. Well, what about the actual course? You're studying ... uh?

K: I'm doing a Masters by coursework in Environmental Studies.

C: Ah, right, and how are you finding that?

K: Yeah, well it's been pretty good really. I've enjoyed the course, but I feel there hasn't been enough contact with the <u>lecturers. They all seem to be</u> Q4
<u>incredibly busy.</u> The only chance I've really had to talk to them was on the field trip.

C: Well that's no good. Could anything be done to improve the course, in your opinion?

K: Well ... I think it would be helpful to have <u>meetings with lecturers</u> on the Q5
course. Say once a fortnight – something like that.

C: Regular meetings. Yes, that could certainly help. Now Kate, we'll come back to you in a minute, but I'd just like to ask Luki some questions.

- -

C: Luki. Where are you from?

L: I am from Indonesia.

C: And how did *you* find Cambridge when you first arrived?

L: Well, I like it here. I think the city is very beautiful.

C: What about your accommodation? Was that OK?

L: Yes, OK. At first <u>I stayed with a family</u> for three months. They were very Q6
kind to me but they had three young children and I found it <u>difficult to</u> Q7
<u>study.</u>

C: Right, I see.

L: So after three months I moved out and now I live with two other students in a <u>student house</u>. It's much cheaper and we like it there. Q8

C: Good, and what about your studies? What are you studying?

L: I'm doing a <u>Bachelor of Computing.</u> Q9

C: Computing. I see. Um, apart from the language difficulties, if you can separate them, how have you found the course?

L: OK, but ...

C: Yes, go on.

L: Well, the main difficulty for me is getting time on the computers in the computer room. It's always busy and this makes it very hard to do my practical work.

C: Yes, I'm sure it would. Can you reserve time in the computer room?

L: No, you can't ... but it would certainly help if we *could* <u>reserve computer</u> Q10
<u>time.</u>

C: Yes. I'll look into that and see if something can't be done to improve things over there. Now let's go back to Kate ...

SECTION 2

Radio presenter:
Well, last week we talked about buying camping equipment and today I'd like to talk to you about buying a bicycle. A simple enough exercise, you might imagine, but there are lots of things to look out for to make sure you get the best deal for your money.

    Well, the range of bicycles is enormous – there are racing bikes, touring bikes, <u>mountain bikes</u> or just plain ordinary bikes for riding round town. They vary enormously in two basic ways: price and <u>quality</u>. This means that the choice you make will probably be determined by the amount of money you want to pay, your own personal needs, what is actually available or a compromise of all three things. However, in broad terms you can spend anything from $50 to <u>$2,000</u> on a bike, so you'll need to know what you are looking for.

    Single speed cycles – that is bikes with no gears, are really only suited to <u>short, casual rides</u>. Their attraction is their simplicity and reliability. After years of neglect they still manage to function, though not always too efficiently. If it's basic transport you're after, then you can't go wrong.

    Three speed cycles on the other hand are all that is really necessary for most <u>town riding, going to the shops and things like that</u>. Like the single speed bike, they are simple and reliable. If you are going to be going up and down lots of hills, then you'll probably want something more efficient.

    Five and ten speed bicycles are best suited to riding over long distances or hilly terrain and to <u>serious touring</u>, so if it's serious touring you're interested in, get a five or ten speed bike. However, it's worth remembering that the <u>difference in price between a five and ten speed cycle is usually very little</u> and so it's well worth paying that little bit extra to get the ten speed one. So I would tend to recommend the ten speed bike as the <u>price is similar</u> – however you'll be getting <u>better quality components</u>.

    Now the next thing we need to look at is size. Buying a cycle is like <u>buying clothes</u>, first of all you find the right size and then you try it on to see if it fits. Contrary to what you might imagine, the size of the cycle is not determined by the size of the wheels, (except in children's cycles), but by the size of the <u>frame</u>. So you'll need to measure the length of your legs and arms to get a frame that is the right size for you.

    Well, that's all from Helpful Hints for today ...

Q11
Q12

Q13

Q14

Q15

Q16

Q17

Q18

Q19

Q20

SECTION 3

F = Fiona
M = Martin

F: Hi there, Martin. How are you going with your Australian studies tutorial paper?
M: Oh good. I've finished it actually.
F: Lucky you. What did you do it on? I'm still trying to find an interesting topic.

M: Well ... after some consideration I decided to look at the history of banana growing in Australia.

F: *(surprised)* Banana growing!

M: Yes, banana growing.

F: *(sarcastically)* Fascinating, I'm sure!   *Q21*

M: Well ... it's not as boring as you'd think. And I wanted to tie it in to the work I've been doing on primary industries and the economy. Anyway I bet there are a few things you didn't know about bananas!

F: Such as?

M: Such as the fact that bananas were among the first plants ever to be domesticated.

F: Oh, really?

M: Yes, they're an extremely nourishing food.   *Q22*

F: I suppose you're going to tell me the whole history of banana growing now, aren't you?

M: Well, it'd be a good practice run for my tutorial next week. I'll do the same   *Q23*
for you some time.

F: OK. Fire away. So where were these bananas first domesticated?

M: According to my research, the Cavendish banana, which is a type of banana and the first type to be cultivated here, actually originated in China but they had a fairly roundabout route before they got to Australia.

F: You mean they didn't go straight from China to Australia?

M: No, they didn't. It seems that in 1826, bananas were taken from South China to England.

F: I suppose they would have made a welcome addition to the English diet.

M: Yes, I'm sure. Well apparently there was an English Duke who was particularly fond of bananas and he used to cultivate them in his hothouse, which is where you have to grow them in England, of course, because of the cool climate and they became quite popular in the UK. So he was the one   *Q24*
responsible for cultivating the Cavendish banana which was then introduced into Australia.

F: I see. And we've been growing them ever since?

M: Yes.

F: Are they hard to grow?

M: Well, yes and no. To grow them in your garden, no, not really. But to grow them commercially you need to know what you're doing. You see, you only get one bunch of bananas per tree and it can take up to three years for a tree   *Q25*
to bear fruit, if you don't do anything special to it. But this period is greatly reduced with modern growing methods, particularly in plantations where you have perfect tropical conditions.

F: Right! So what are you looking at? One year? Two years?

M: No, no, around 15 months in good conditions for a tree to produce a bunch of   *Q26*
bananas. And once you've got your bunch you cut the bunch and the plant down.

F: So how do the trees reproduce then?

M: Well, bananas are normally grown from suckers which spring up around the parent plant, usually just above the plant. They tend to like to grow uphill –   *Q27*
or at least that's the common wisdom.

F: So that's why banana plantations are <u>usually on hillsides</u>, is it?

M: Yes. They grow best like that.

F: That's interesting!

M: If you plant them in rich soil and give them <u>plenty of water</u> at the beginning   *Q28*
of summer, then they should be well advanced by the beginning of winter
when growth virtually stops. But in a country like England, they're hard to
grow, although you *can* grow them in a hothouse.

F: But in Australia, it's not difficult?

M: No, though even here, <u>the growers put plastic bags around the bunches to</u>   *Q29*
<u>protect them</u> and keep them warm. If you go up to the banana growing
districts, you'll see all these banana trees with plastic bags on them.

F: But how do they stop the bananas going bad before they reach the shops?

M: Well, the banana bunches are picked well before the fruit is ripe. Once you
cut the bunch, the bananas stop growing but they do continue to ripen. The
interesting thing is that once one banana ripens, <u>it gives off a gas which then</u>
<u>helps all the others to ripen</u> so they pretty much all ripen within a few hours   *Q30*
of each other.

F: Amazing! So do we export lots of bananas overseas, to Europe and Asia for
instance?

M: Well, oddly enough, no. I believe <u>New Zealand</u> takes a small proportion of   *Q31 or 32*
the crop but otherwise <u>they're mostly grown for the domestic market</u>, which   *Q32 or 31*
is surprising when you think about it because we grow an enormous number
of bananas each year.

F: Yes, well – thank you for all that information. I'm sure the tutorial paper will
go really well – you certainly seem to have done your research on the subject.

M: Let's hope so.

SECTION 4

J   = John
D   = Diane Greenbaum

J: Good morning, good morning, everyone, and welcome to our regular lecture
on health issues. This series of lectures is organised by the Students' Union
and is part of the union's attempt to help you, the students of this university,
<u>to stay healthy</u> while coping with study and social life at the same time. So   *Q33*
it's a great pleasure for me to welcome back Ms Diane Greenbaum who is <u>a</u>
<u>professional dietician</u> and who has been kind enough to give up her time, in   *Q34*
what I know is a very hectic schedule, to come along and talk to us today.

D: Thank you. Thank you very much, John. May I say it's a pleasure to be
back. Now, stresses at university, being away from home and having to look
after yourselves, learning your way around the campus all contribute to
making it quite hard sometimes to ensure that your diet is adequate. So
today I'm going to talk about <u>ways of making sure that you eat well while at</u>
<u>the same time staying within your budget.</u>   *Q35*

- -

If you have a well balanced diet, then you should be getting all the vitamins that you need for normal daily living. However, sometimes we think we're eating the right foods but the <u>vitamins are escaping, perhaps as a result of cooking</u> and anyway we're not getting the full benefit of them. Now, if you lack vitamins in any way, the solution isn't to rush off and take vitamin pills, though they can sometimes help. No, it's far better to look at your diet and how you prepare your food.

Q36

So what are vitamins? Well, the dictionary tells us they are 'food factors essential in small quantities to maintain life'. Now, there are fat soluble vitamins which can be stored for quite some time by the body and there are water soluble vitamins which <u>are removed more rapidly from the body and so a regular daily intake</u> of these ones is needed.

Q37

OK, so how can you ensure that your diet contains enough of the vitamins you need? Well, first of all, you may have to establish some new eating habits! No more chips at the uni canteen, I'm afraid! Now firstly, you must <u>eat a variety of foods</u>. Then you need to ensure that you eat at least four servings of fruit and vegetables daily. Now you'll need to shop two or three times a week to make sure that they're fresh, and store your vegetables <u>in the fridge or in a cool, dark place.</u>

Q38

Q39

Now let's just refresh our memories by looking at the Healthy Diet Pyramid. OK, can you all see that? Good. Well, now, as you see, we've got three levels to our pyramid. At the top in the smallest area are the things which we should really be <u>trying to avoid</u> as much as possible. Things like ... yes, sugar, salt, butter ... all that sort of thing.

Example

Next, on the middle of our pyramid we find the things that we can <u>eat in moderation</u>. Not too much though! And that's where we find milk, lean meat, fish, nuts, eggs. And then at the bottom of the pyramid are the things that you can <u>eat lots of</u>! Because they're the things that are really good for you. And here we have bread, vegetables and fruit. So don't lose sight of your healthy diet pyramid when you do your shopping.

Q40

Q41

PRACTICE TEST 3

SECTION 1

M = Male student
F = Female student
C = Clerk

M: How do *you* come to the university each day? Train or bus or do you have a car?

F: Oh, <u>I always walk</u> – I haven't got a car and anyway I live quite close.
   Repeat

Example

M: Do you know anything about parking rights on the campus? I was wondering whether students are allowed to park their cars on the campus or not?

F: Yes, I think <u>it's possible for post graduate students but not for</u>   *Q1*
      <u>undergraduate students.</u>
M: That doesn't seem very fair.
F: No, I suppose not, but there simply isn't enough room on the campus for
      everyone to park.
M: Do you need a parking permit?
F: Yeah, I believe you do.
M: Where do I get that from?
F: I think you can get a parking sticker from the administration office.
M: Where's that?
F: It's in the building called <u>Block G</u>. Right next to Block E.   *Q2*
M: Block G?
F: Yeah.
M: Oh right. And what happens to you if you don't buy a sticker? Do they
      clamp your wheels or give you a fine?
F: No, I think <u>they tow your car away.</u>   *Q3*
M: Oh really?
F: Yeah. <u>And then they fine you as well</u> because you have to pay to get the car   *Q3*
      back.
M: I'd better get the sticker then.
F: Yeah.
M: Where exactly is the administration office again? I'm new to this university
      and I'm still trying to find my way around.
F: Right. You go along Library Road, past the tennis courts on your left and
      the swimming pool on your right and the administration office is opposite
      the car park on the left. You can't miss it.
M: <u>So it's up Library Road, past the swimming pool, opposite the car park.</u>   *Q4*
      Right, I'll go straight over there. Bye and thanks for the help.

- -

C: Good morning, can I help you?
M: Yes, I was told to come over here to get a parking sticker. Is this the right
      place?
C: Yes, it is. Are you a post graduate student?
M: Yes, I am.
C: OK, well, I'll just need to take some details ... Your name?
M: <u>Richard Lee – that's spelt L double E.</u>   *Q5*
C: Richard ... Lee. And the address?
M: Flat 13, <u>30 Enmore Road</u>   *Q6*
C: How do you spell Enmore?
M: <u>E-N-M-O-R-E.</u> And that's in the suburb of <u>Newport: N-E-W-P-O-R-T.</u>   *Q7*
C: Faculty?
M: I beg your pardon?
C: Which faculty are you in?
M: <u>Architecture, the Faculty of Architecture.</u>   *Q8*
C: Right ... and the registration number of your car?
M: Let me see um L X J five oh ... No, sorry, I always get that wrong, it's
      <u>LJX 058K.</u>   *Q9*
C: LJX 508K.

M: No ... 058K.
C: Ah. And what make is the car?
M: <u>It's a Ford.</u>   *Q10*
C: A Ford. Fine! Well, I'll just get you to sign here and when you've paid the
    cashier I'll be able to issue you with the sticker.
M: Right. Where do I pay?
C: Just across the corridor in the cashier's office. Oh, but it's 12.30 now and
    they close at 12.15 for lunch. But <u>they open again at a quarter past two</u> until   *Q11*
    4.30.
M: Oh ... they're not open till quarter past two?
C: No. When you get your sticker, you must attach it to the <u>front windscreen</u> of   *Q12*
    your car. I'm afraid it's not valid if you don't have it stuck on the window.
M: Right, I see. Thanks very much. I'll just wait here then.

SECTION 2

Guide:
Good morning, everyone, and welcome to the Maritime Museum.
   Now before we commence our tour I'd just like to tell you a little bit about the
history of the museum. As you can see, it's a very modern building built in the
post modern style and it was in fact opened by the Prime Minister of Australia in
<u>November 1991.</u> It's been designed with a nautical flavour in mind to remind us of   *Q13*
our links with the sea. But the museum isn't only housed in this building; there are
a number of <u>historic ships docked outside in the harbour which form part of the</u>   *Q14*
<u>museum</u> and which you are also free to visit, and we'll be coming to them shortly.
   I'd just like to point out one or two things of general interest while we're here.
Handicapped toilets are located on this floor and <u>the door shows a wheelchair.</u>   *Example*
The cloakroom where you can hang your coat or leave your bags is just behind us
here. The education centre is on the top floor and there's a good little library in
there which you might like to use. Follow the signs to the Education Centre –
you'll see a lot of little <u>green arrows</u> on the wall. The green arrows will take you   *Q15*
there. The information desk, marked with the small letter **i** on your plan is located
right here in the foyer, so if you get separated from your friends, I suggest you
<u>make your way back to the information desk</u> because we'll be returning to this   *Q16*
spot at the end of the tour. All right?
   Now, if you look out this window you should be able to see where the
museum's ships are docked. If you want to go on a tour of the old ship, the
Vampire, she's docked over there and you should meet outside on the quay.
However, a word of warning! I don't recommend it for the grandmas and
grandpas because there are <u>lots of stairs</u> to climb. Right, now, let's move on.   *Q17*
Oh, I almost forgot to give you the times for that tour. Now, tours of the *Vampire*
run <u>on the hour, every hour.</u> All right?   *Q18*

   Let's take a walk round the museum now. The first room we're coming to is the
theatre. This room is used to screen videos of special interest and we also use it for
lectures. There's a continuous video showing today about the voyages of <u>Captain</u>

Cook, so come back here later on if you want to learn more about Captain Cook.   *Q19*

Now, we're moving along the gallery known as the Leisure Gallery. This is one of our permanent exhibitions and here we try to give you an idea of the many different ways in which Australians have enjoyed their time by the sea: surfing, swimming, lifesaving clubs, that's all very much a part of Australian culture. At the   *Q20* end of this section we'll come to the Picture Gallery where we've got a marvellous collection of paintings, all by Australian artists. I think you can buy reproductions   *Q21* of some of these paintings in the museum shop. Well worth a good look.

Now we're coming to the Members' Lounge. As a member of the museum you would be entitled to use the members' lounge for refreshments. Membership costs $50 a year or $70 for all the family. So it's quite good value because entry to the   *Q22* museum is then free.

And down at the far end of this floor, you'll find the section which we've called *Passengers and the Sea*. In this part of the museum we've gathered together a wonderful collection of souvenirs from the old days when people travelled by ship.   *Q23* You'll find all sorts of things there: old suitcases, ships' crockery, first class cabins decorated in the fashion of the day. Just imagine what it must have been like to travel first class.

Now I'm going to leave you to walk round the museum on your own for a while and we'll all meet back again at the information desk in three quarters of an hour's time. I hope you enjoy your time with us at the museum today. Thank you.

SECTION 3

T = Tutor
M = Mark
S = Susan

T: OK, everybody, good morning! It's Mark's turn to talk to us today, so Mark, I'll ask you to get straight down to business.

M: Right!

T: Now following on from what we were discussing last week in Susan's tutorial on approaches to marketing, you were going to give us a quick run down on a new strategy for pricing which is now being used by many large companies   *Q24* known as 'revenue management' ... before we go on to your actual tutorial paper on Sales Targets. Is that correct?

M: Yeah, OK, well ...

T: So what exactly is revenue management?

M: Well, it's a way of managing your pricing by treating things like airline tickets and hotel rooms rather more as if they were perishable goods.

S: Yeah, I just tried to book a ticket yesterday for Perth and would you believe there are three different prices for the flight?

M: Right! And what was the rationale for that?

S: Well ... the travel agent said it depended on when you book and the length of the stay, like it's cheap if you stay away for a Saturday night, presumably because this isn't business travel, and even cheaper if you buy a ticket where   *Q25* you can't get a refund if you have to cancel; in that case the ticket costs about half the price. You wouldn't think it would make that much difference, would you?

M: Well it does, and that's basically because the airlines are now treating their seats like a commodity. You see – if you want a seat today, then you pay far more for it than if you want it in three weeks' time.

S: That seems rather unfair.

M: Well ... not really ... when you think about it, that's just common sense isn't it?　　　*Q26*

S: I suppose so.

T: What this actually means is that in the same row of seats on the same flight you could have three people who have all paid a different price for their tickets.

S: And is this just happening in Australia?

M: No, no it's the same all over the world. Airlines are able to 'market' a seat as a perishable product, with different values at different stages of its life.

S: Well like mangoes or apples at the market.

M: Yeah, it's exactly like that. The fact is that the companies are not actually interested in selling you a cheap flight! They're interested in selling the seats and flying aeroplanes that are full.　　　*Q27*

T: Mark, why do you think revenue management has come about?

M: Well, as far as I can see, there are two basic reasons: firstly because the law has been changed to allow the companies to do this. You see in the past they didn't have the right to keep changing the prices of the tickets, and secondly we now have very powerful computer programs to do the calculations and so the prices can be changed at a moment's notice.　　　*Q28* *Q29*

S: So you mean ten minutes could be critical when you're buying a plane ticket?

M: Absolutely!

T: That's right!

M: And I understand we have almost reached the stage where these computer programs that the airlines are using will eventually be available to consumers to find the best deals for their travel plans from their home computer.　　　*Q30*

S: Heavens! What a thought! So the travel agent could easily become a thing of the past if you could book your airline tickets from home. Are there any other industries using this system, or is it restricted to the airline business?

M: Many of the big hotel groups are doing it now. That's why the price of a bed in a hotel can also vary so much ... depending on when and where you book it.　　　*Q31*

T: It's all a bit of a gamble really.

M: Yes, and hire car companies are also using revenue management to set their tariffs, because they are also dealing with a 'commodity' if you like ... so the cost of hiring a car will depend on demand.　　　*Q32*

T: Well, thank you, Mark, for that overview ... that was well researched. Now let's get on with your main topic for today ...

SECTION 4

Marketing Consultant:
Good morning. Welcome to this talk on *Space Management*. And today I'm going to look particularly at space management in the supermarket.

Now since the time supermarkets began, marketing consultants, like us, have been gathering information about customers' shopping habits.

To date, various research methods have been used to help promote the sales of supermarket products. There is, for example, the simple and direct <u>questionnaire which provides information from customers about their views on displays and products</u> and then helps retailers make decisions about what to put where.

Example
Q33

Another method to help managers understand just how shoppers go around their stores are the <u>hidden television cameras</u> that film us as we shop and monitor our physical movement around the supermarket aisles: where do we start, what do we buy last, what attracts us, etc.

Q34

More sophisticated techniques now include video surveillance and such devices as the <u>eye movement recorder</u>. This is a device which shoppers volunteer to wear taped into a headband, and which traces their eye movements as they walk round the shop recording the most eye-catching areas of shelves and aisles.

Q35

But with today's technology, *Space Management* is now a highly sophisticated method of manipulating the way we shop to ensure maximum profit. Supermarkets are able to invest millions of pounds in powerful computers which tell them what sells best and where.

Now, an example of this is *Spaceman* which is a computer program that helps the retailer to decide which particular product sells best in which part of the store. Now Spaceman works by receiving information from the electronic checkouts (where customers pay) on <u>how well a product is selling in a particular position.</u> *Spaceman* then suggests the most profitable combination of <u>an article and its position in the store.</u>

Q36

Q37

- -

So, let's have a look at what we know about supermarkets and the way people behave when they walk down the aisles and take the articles they *think* they need from the shelves.

Now here's a diagram of one supermarket aisle and two rows of shelves. Here's the *entrance* at the top left-hand corner.

Now products placed *here*, at the beginning of aisles, don't sell well. In tests, secret fixed cameras have filmed shoppers' movements around a store over a seven-day period. When the film is speeded up, it clearly shows that <u>we walk straight past these areas</u> on our way to the centre of an aisle. Items placed here just don't attract people.

Q38

When we finally stop at the centre of an aisle, we pause and take stock, casting our eyes along the length of it. Now products displayed here sell well and <u>do even better if they are placed at eye level</u> so that the customer's eyes hit upon them instantly. Products here are snapped up and manufacturers pay a lot for these shelf areas which are known in the trade as <u>hotspots</u>. Naturally everyone wants their products to be in a hotspot.

Q39

Q40

But the prime positions in the store are the ends of the aisles, otherwise known as *Gondola ends*. Now these stand out and grab our attention. For this reason new products are launched in these positions and manufacturers are charged widely varying prices for this privileged spot. Also, the end of an aisle may be used for <u>promoting special offers</u> which are frequently found waiting for us as we turn the corner of an aisle.

Q41

Well, now, eventually of course, we have to pay. Any spot where a supermarket can be sure we are going to stand still and concentrate for more than a few seconds is good for sales. That's why the shelves at the checkout have long been a favourite for manufacturers of <u>chocolates</u> – perhaps the most sure-fire 'impulse' food of all.

Q42

PRACTICE TEST 4

SECTION 1

F = Female student
M = Male student
C = Clerk

F: Excuse me. Can you help me? I was looking for the <u>Main Hall.</u>
M: Maybe I can, actually. I'm looking for the <u>Main Hall</u>, too. I think it's in the   *Example*
    Administration building. Are you a new student?
F: Yes, I am.
    Repeat
M: I thought you looked as lost as me. I'm trying to find the admin building,
    too, so that I can register for my course. But I don't seem to be having much
    luck.
F: Well, look, according to this map of the campus here, you go <u>straight up the</u>
    <u>steps, turn left and the building is on the right.</u> OK, let's see if we can find it.   *Q1*
M: Oh, this looks right. Oh, yeah, it must be. Look, there are hundreds of other
    people here!
F: There must be <u>at least 50 people</u> in the queue – we'll be here till gone 2   *Q2*
    o'clock at this rate.
M: And I'm starving!
F: So am I.
M: Actually, I was on my way to the canteen to get something for lunch. Why
    don't I go to the canteen and buy something and you stay here and wait?
F: Good idea.
M: What would you like? Pizza, sandwich, hot dog, fried rice. They do
    everything ...
F: Oh, something easy. Take away fried rice sounds good.
M: OK, fried ...
F: No, on second thoughts, <u>I'll have a cheese and tomato sandwich.</u>   *Q3*
M: Right – one cheese and tomato – anything to drink?
F: Yeah, get me a coffee, would you?
M: Oh, hot coffee's a bit hard to carry. What about a coke or an orange juice?

F:	Oh, um … <u>get me an orange juice, then</u>. Look, here's five dollars.	*Q4*
M:	Oh, take two dollars back, it shouldn't cost me more than three dollars.	
F:	Well, <u>keep the five and we'll sort it out later</u>. Oh, and could you get me an apple as well?	*Q5*
M:	OK. Back in a minute.	

F:	Oh, hello. I'm here to register for the First Year Law course.	
C:	I'll just have to fill out this form for our records. What's your name?	
F:	Julia Perkins.	
C:	Can you spell that for me?	
F:	Yeah, that's <u>J-U-L-I-A P-E-R-K-I-N-S</u>.	*Q6*
C:	Address?	
F:	Flat 5, <u>15 Waratah Road, that's W-A-R-A-T-A-H</u>, Brisbane.	*Q7 and Q8*
C:	Brisbane … And your telephone number?	
F:	We haven't got the phone on yet. We've only just moved in.	
C:	OK, well can you let us have the number once the phone's connected and I'll make a note here <u>to be advised</u>. And the course?	*Q9*
F:	I beg your pardon?	
C:	What course are you doing?	
F:	<u>First Year Law</u>.	*Q10*
C:	Right. Well, you'll have to go across to the Law Faculty and get this card stamped and then you come back here with it and pay your union fee.	
F:	Thanks very much.	

M:	Oh, there you are.	
F:	I thought you were never going to come back.	
M:	Sorry! The canteen was absolutely packed and I had to wait for ages. Then when I got to the front of the queue they had hardly any food left. So <u>I had to get you a slice of pizza</u>. I'm sorry.	*Q11*
F:	Oh, that's OK. I could eat anything, I'm so hungry.	
M:	<u>And there's your bottle of orange juice and your apple</u>. At least I managed that.	
F:	Great. Thanks a lot.	
M:	Oh and here's your $2 back.	
F:	Don't worry about it. Buy me a cup of coffee later!	
M:	Oh, alright then! So how'd you go?	
F:	Well in order to register we've got to go to the Law Faculty and get this card stamped and then go back to the Admin building and <u>pay the union fees</u>. That means we're registered. After that we have to go to the notice board to find out about lectures and then we have to put our names down for tutorial groups and go to the library to …	*Q12*
M:	Great. Well first let's sit down and have our lunch.	

SECTION 2

Speaker:
Thanks for turning up today, thanks for turning up today to this short talk I'm
going to give on student banking. Many of you are unfamiliar with the way banks
work in this country and today's talk should just give you a few starting points. I
will, of course, answer any questions at the end.

Right. Well, as you probably know, you'll need to open a bank account while
you're here – it's the safest place to keep your money – and it's best to open an
account with one of the major banks. You should each have a handout with the
names and addresses ... there's *Barclays* in Realty Square, *National Westminster* in   *Example*
Preston Park, *Lloyds* in City Plaza and *Midland* in Hope Street. OK. All these banks   Q13
offer special student accounts. However, it's important to note that as an
international student you'll not necessarily be eligible for all the facilities offered to
resident students.

Now, as an international student, you will need to provide evidence that you can   Q14
fund yourself for however long your course lasts. Banks have different policies and
the services that they'll offer you will depend on your individual circumstances and
on the discretion of the bank manager involved. So it's a matter of going there and
finding out about your own particular situation.

Right, erm, when you do go to open a bank account, you should take some
documentation with you. I've already mentioned that you must be able to support
yourself. In addition to this, most banks ask you to bring your passport and your   Q15
letter or certificate of enrolment. OK?

Now, by far the most useful type of account to open is a current account. When   Q16
you do this, you will actually get what is called a 'student account' which is a
current account with special concessions for students. When you open the account,
the bank will give you a chequebook and you can use this to draw money out   Q17
as you need it. If you need to write cheques in shops, you'll also need a cheque
card. This is really an identity card which guarantees that correctly written cheques
up to the value stated on the card will be honoured by the bank. OK?

- -

Right, er, if you want to draw out cash for yourself you can make the cheque
payable in your own name or 'to cash'. You can also withdraw cash from a
cashpoint machine with a cashcard. These are extremely useful as they enable you
to withdraw cash from your account during the day or at night.   Q18

There is also another card called *Switch* or *Delta* and you can use this to pay for   Q19
things in shops. It takes the money right out of your account, so you don't need
your chequebook.

Now – you may want to take more money out of the bank than you have in it.
This is called having an overdraft. Be very careful with this – you should not do   Q20
this without permission from your bank. Overdrafts usually incur charges, though
some banks offer interest-free overdrafts to some students. But find out before you
get one! Right?

Well, that just leaves opening times – when can you go? Banks used to be open
from 9.30 am until 3.30 pm from Monday to Friday but many main branches are   Q21
now open until 4.30 or 5 pm on weekdays and some of the bigger branches in

London and other major cities are now open for a limited time on Saturdays. OK – any questions?

SECTION 3

I = Ilmar
D = Dawn

I: Hi, Dawn.
D: Oh hi, Ilmar.
I: I'm glad I've bumped into you. I've just found a great idea for the presentation we've got to do for Dr Banks next month.
D: What, the one on everyday objects?
I: Yes ... look at this article ... it's really interesting.
D: The aluminium coke can?
I: You know ... coca cola cans, soft drink cans. Look let's sit down here. Have you got a minute?
D: Sure ... I'll just get my bag.
D: OK, so you think we can get a presentation out of this article?
I: I'm sure we can. First of all we can provide some interesting facts about the aluminium cans that we drink out of every day.
D: Like ... ?
I: Well, here ... it says that in the US they produce <u>300 million</u> aluminium drink cans each day.   *Q22*
D: Wow! 300 million!
I: Exactly. That's an enormous number. It says here 'outstrips the production of nails or <u>paper clips</u>'. And they say that the manufacturers of these cans exercise as much attention and precision in producing them as aircraft manufacturers do when they make the wing of an aircraft!   *Q23*
D: Really! Let's have a look.
I: They're trying to produce the perfect can – as thin but as strong as possible.
D: Mmm ... this bit's interesting ... 'today's can weighs about 0.48 ounces: <u>thinner than two pieces of paper ... from this magazine say.</u>'   *Q24*
I: Yeah, and yet it can take a lot of weight.
D: More than 90 pounds of pressure per square inch – <u>three times the pressure of a car tyre.</u> OK, I agree, it's a good topic.   *Q25*

I: What I thought was that we could do a large picture of a coke can and label it and then talk about the different parts. Look, I've done a rough picture here.
D: OK, so where shall we start?
I: Well, the *lid* is complicated. Let's start with the *body* first. I'll do a line from the centre of the can ... like this ... and label it *'body'*. What does it say?
D: It's made of aluminium, of course, and it's <u>thicker at the bottom.</u>   *Q26*
I: Right, so that it can take all that pressure.

D: And then I think you should draw another line from the body for the *label*.

I: Right 'label'. The aluminium is ironed out until it's so thin that it produces ... what does it say?   *Q27*

D: 'A reflective surface suitable for decoration.'

I: That's right, apparently it helps advertisers, too.

D: Yes, because it's so attractively decorated.

I: Good ... and then there's the *base*.

D: Yes, it says <u>the bottom of the can is shaped like a dome</u> so that it can resist the internal pressure.   *Q28*

I: That's interesting. I didn't know that.

D: Nor did I. OK, so going up to the *lid* ... there are several things we can label here. There's the rim around the edge which seals the can.

I: Got that. <u>And there's a funny word for the seal, isn't there?</u>

D: <u>Yes, it's a flange.</u>   *Q29*

I: What does it say about it?

D: Well, the can's filled with coke or whatever and after that the top of the can is trimmed and then bent over to secure the lid.

I: That's right, it looks like a seam. We could even do a blow-up of it like this ... F–L–A–N–G–E ...

D: Yes, that would be clearer. I think we should label the *lid* itself and say that it constitutes <u>twenty-five percent of the total weight.</u>   *Q30*

I: Twenty-five percent ... so it's stronger than the body of the can.

D: So to save money, manufacturers make it smaller than the rest of the can!

I: Didn't know that either ... so how do we open a can of coke?

D: Mmm ... first of all there's the *tab* which we pull up to open the can and that's held in place by a *rivet*.

I: Mmm ... I think that's too small for us to include.

D: I agree, but we can talk about it in the presentation. <u>We *can* show the *opening* though</u>.   *Q31*

I: That's the bit of the can that drops down into the drink when we pull the tab.

D: Yeah, hopefully. Sometimes the tab just breaks off.

I: I know.

D: Anyway the opening is scored so that it pushes in easily but doesn't detach itself.

I: OK, we can show that by drawing a shadow of it inside the can, like this. <u>I'll</u> label it *scored opening*. Great ... well, I think we've got the basis of a really interesting presentation. Let's go and photocopy the article.

D: Fine. I'll take it home and study it some more.

SECTION 4

Lecturer:

Good morning and welcome to the University's Open Day and to our mini-lecture from the Sports Studies department. Now the purpose of this lecture is twofold: one – <u>we want you to experience a university lecture</u>, to give you a taste of what *Q32* listening to a university lecture is like, and two – <u>we want you to find out</u> *Q33* <u>something about the Sports Studies program</u> at this university. So feel free to ask any questions during the talk and I'll do my best to answer them.

Right – so what *does* a course in Sports Studies involve? Well, you wouldn't be blamed for not knowing the answer to this question because Sports Studies as a discipline is still comparatively new. But it's a growing area and one which is now firmly established at our university.

Now there are three distinct strands to Sports Studies and you would need to choose fairly early on just which direction you wanted to follow. And I'll just run over these now. Firstly, we've got the Sports Psychology strand, <u>secondly, we've</u> *Q34* <u>got the Sports Management strand</u>, and last, but not least, there's the Sports Physiology strand. So just to recap there's Sports Psychology, Sports Management, and Sports Physiology.

Let's look first at Psychology. <u>Now the people who study Sports Psych want to</u> *Q35* <u>work with top athletes</u>, and they're looking at what will take those athletes that one percent extra. <u>What makes them win?</u> When all other things are equal, *Q36* physically all other things are equal, they want to know … what are the mental factors involved? The Sports Psychologist works closely with the athlete through his or her training program and becomes an integral part of the team. In fact you could say that they play just as important a role as the coach. So if you're interested in what makes people win, this could be the area for you.

Now secondly, we've got the strand which I referred to as Sports Management and this goes hand in hand with the area of Sports Marketing. So you might like to think of this area as having two branches: Management and Marketing. On the Management side we look at issues relating to the running of sports clubs, management of athletes, that sort of thing. But then on the other side, we've got Sports Marketing. And this is the side that interests me more because <u>here we will</u> *Q37* <u>look at the market forces behind sport</u>. Questions like: why do people spend their money on a football match, or a tennis game, rather than, say, on buying a CD or going to the cinema? What are those market forces?

Sport used to just compete with sport. Nowadays it competes <u>with other leisure</u> <u>activities</u>. The spectators go to sport to be entertained rather than out of loyalty to *Q38* a team. They want to have an evening out and they don't want the cheap seats any more; they want good seats, <u>they want entertainment</u>. And the professional *Q39* sportsmen and women respond to this without question. They're there to give a performance. They provide the entertainment. So in the marketing course we address all these commercial issues and we look at how this hooks back into the Management of sport.

<u>Now the third branch</u> of Sports Studies sometimes comes under another name and <u>is also known as Exercise Science</u>. And again here we find that there are two *Q40* distinct types of exercise science. The first is working very much at the macro level. What I call the huffing and puffing people. So <u>this looks at fitness testing, body</u>

measurements, all that sort of thing. But the more interesting side of sports physiology, at least in my view, is the side that looks at the micro level, looking at cellular change. They're doing cellular research, looking at changes in body cells when the body is under stress.

Q41

Q42

So that just about brings us to the end of our mini-lecture for today. I hope you've found it interesting and I look forward to seeing you all on our course next year. Feel free to come and talk to me if you want any more information. I'll be over at that notice board near the main entrance.

Answer keys

LISTENING

Section 1

1	A
2	C
3	D
4	D
5	C
6	Prescott *(must be correct spelling with capital 'P')*
7	41
8	Fountain *(must have capital 'F')*
9	752239
10	£65

Section 2

11	E	*in*
12	F	*any*
13	H	*order*
14	$250 million	
15	roads//road system	
16	too late	
17	school children//boys	
18	3	
19	boats//pleasure craft//boats and pleasure craft	
20	pilot	
21	(musical) instruments	

Section 3

22	A
23	B
24	C
25	A
26	talk//give a talk
27	write up work
28	can choose
29	open book
30	closed reserve
31	vocational (subjects)//(preparing for) work/employment

Section 4

32	B
33	C
34	history and economics
35	(meeting) deadlines (for essays)
36	attendance
37	B
38	C
39	B
40	D
41	A

PRACTICE TEST 1

READING

READING PASSAGE 1   *A spark, a flint: How fire leapt to life*

Questions	Task	Skills tested
1–8	Gap-fill summary	• skimming for information • detailed understanding of a section of text • ability to paraphrase/re-word original text
9–15	Matching (items to descriptions)	• skimming for specific information • understanding description/characteristics • understanding paraphrase

Questions 1–8

Question	Answer
1	preserve
2	unaware
3	chance
4	friction
5	rotating
6	percussion
7	Eskimos
8	despite

Questions 9–15

Suggested approach

- Read the task rubric carefully. In this task you have to decide which match is being described in each question.
- Decide what information is best to skim for in the passage: the *type of match* or the *description*. In this question it is best to skim for the types of match as these are names, some of which are in italics; they are easier for you to pick out.
- Skim through the text until you find match A, the *Ethereal Match.*
- Read that section of the text and underline any important features of this match.
- Read through the descriptions and write A next to any that fit this type of match. If you

think there is more than one possible description for the match, note A next to both. (The rubric states that you may use any match more than once.)

- Towards the top of the second page of the text it states that the Ethereal Match consisted of a 'sealed glass tube', so A is the answer to question 14. Note that the description is expressed differently from the text. Sometimes you have to match the meaning rather than the words.
- If you think none of the descriptions fits this type of match, go on to the next; the rubric also states that there are not enough descriptions to fit all the matches.

Question	Answer	Location of answer in text
9	F	'... the red phosphorus was non-toxic'
10	D	'... three years later it was copied ...'
11	E	'... since white phosphorus is a deadly poison ...'
12	C	'The first matches resembling those used today ...'
13	G	'... a brewery had the novel idea of advertising ...'
14	A	'... a sealed glass tube ...'
15	C	'... borrowed the formula from a military rocket-maker ...'

READING PASSAGE 2   *Zoo conservation programmes*

Questions	Task	Skills tested
16–22	Yes, No, Not Given	• skimming for detailed information • identifying attitude and opinion • understanding gist and paraphrase
23–25	Multiple choice	• skimming for factual information • identifying main and supporting points • understanding attitude
26–28	Selecting factors	• skimming/scanning for specific information • identifying main ideas • understanding paraphrase and inference

Questions 16–25

Question	Answer
16	YES
17	YES
18	NOT GIVEN
19	NO
20	NO
21	NOT GIVEN
22	YES
23	B
24	C
25	A

Questions 26–28

Suggested approach

• Read the task rubric carefully. Only *three* of the factors in the list are correct. The correct factors explain why the author *doubts the value* of the WZCS document.

• Scan the text and mark the section that discusses the accuracy/value of the WZCS document. This is from the third paragraph onwards.

• Read through the list of factors to familiarise yourself with it.

• Begin reading the third paragraph more carefully, looking for phrases that signal that the writer is going to discuss something that is wrong with the document. The first signal is: 'This is probably the document's *first failing* ...' You can infer from what the writer

then states, that **A** is one of the correct factors.

• Re-read the list of factors from B–F.

• Continue reading the text, looking for other signals.

• Select the two other correct factors. Remember that if you put more than one factor beside each question number on your answer sheet, you will not get any marks. However, the three correct answers can be written down in any order.

Question	Answer		Location of answer in text
26	A	*in*	'... 10,000 is a serious underestimate of the total number of places masquerading as zoological establishments.'
27	D	*any*	'One would assume that the calibre of these institutions would have been carefully examined but ...'
28	E	*order*	The last two paragraphs of the text, but in particular: 'Today approximately 16 species might be said to have been 'saved' by captive breeding programmes, although a number of these can hardly be looked upon as resounding successes.'

READING PASSAGE 3   *Architecture*

Questions	Task	Skills tested
29–35	Completing a table	• following a chronological account • skimming for specific information • noting main ideas
36–40	Matching (causes to effects)	• skimming/scanning for information • understanding cause and effect relationships • understanding paraphrase

Questions 29–35

Question	Answer
29	timber and stone
30	Modernism
31	International style
32	badly designed buildings//multi-storey housing//mass-produced, low-cost high-rises
33	preservation
34	High-Tech
35	co-existence of styles//different styles together//styles mixed

Questions 36–40

Suggested approach
- Read the task rubric carefully. You have to decide which *effect* arose from each *cause.*
- Decide which list you should work from. In this case it is better to work from List A as you must find an effect in List B for every question. The causes also come first chronologically in the cause/effect relationship: List B contains *results* of List A.
- Read through List B to familiarise yourself with it.
- Read item 36.
- Skim through the passage until you locate the information in the text.
- Read this section of the text in detail noting any *effects* of **36**.
- Read through List B again.
- Select the effect of question 36. If you think there is more than one effect, mark both and

come back to this item later. But remember that only one answer is correct.
- In the third paragraph it states that the increase in urban populations 'helped to turn parts of cities into slums'. So the answer to question 36 is G.
- Repeat this procedure with items 37–40.

Question	Answer	Location of answer in text
36	G	'Such rapid and uncontrolled growth helped to turn parts of cities into slums.'
37	F	'These were stripped of unnecessary decoration that would detract from their primary purpose – to be used or lived in.'
38	H	'But the economic depression ... prevented their ideas from being widely realised until the economic conditions improved ...'
39	C	'Many of these buildings ... have since been demolished.'
40	D	'They originated in the US ... to help meet the demand for more economical use of land.'

PRACTICE TEST 2

LISTENING KEYS

Section 1

1 student accommodation/hostel
2 awful food
3 not friendly//kept to themselves *(do not accept 'lonely')*
4 lecturers (too) busy
5 regular meetings//meetings with lecturers//fortnightly meetings
6 family//homestay
7 lot of noise//children made noise//difficult to study
8 student house
9 (Bachelor of) Computing
10 reserve computer time

Section 2

11 mountain
12 quality
13 $2,000
14 short/casual rides
15 town riding//shopping
16 serious touring
17 similar//almost the same
18 better quality (components)
19 buying clothes
20 frame

Section 3

21 B
22 C
23 D
24 B
25 one bunch
26 15 months
27 uphill//on hillsides
28 lots of/plenty of water
29 plastic bags
30 bananas/ones (to) ripen
31 C } *either*
32 D } *way round*

Section 4

33 B
34 D
35 C
36 cooking
37 (regular) daily intake
38 (a) variety
39 the dark//the fridge//a cool place//a dark place
40 eat in moderation//not too much
41 eat lots//eat most

READING

READING PASSAGE 1   *Right and left-handedness in humans*

Questions	Task	Skills tested
1–7	Matching (people to opinions)	• skimming/scanning for information • understanding gist and paraphrase
8–10	Completing a table	• skimming for factual information
11–12	Multiple choice	• skimming/scanning for information • identifying main and supporting points • understanding paraphrase • making inferences

Questions 1–7

Suggested approach

- Read the task rubric carefully. You have to match the *opinions* with the *people* who express them in the text.
- Read through the list of opinions to familiarise yourself with it.
- In this case it is probably best to skim through the text looking for names as these are easy to identify. So skim through the text until you come to the first name: Professor Turner.
- The text states in the first paragraph that Professor Turner has studied left-handedness. It goes on to say that he noted a 'distinctive asymmetry' in the human population.
- Skim through the list of opinions again. Number 7 states 'Asymmetry is a common feature of the human body.' So the answer to question 7 is E.
- Continue this procedure with the rest of the text. Note that the opinions in the questions are expressed differently from the text. This is known as 'paraphrasing'. It means that you will have to match the *meaning* rather than the exact words.

Question	Answer	Location of answer in text
1	B	'... evolution of speech went with right-handed preference.'
2	D	gist of final paragraph
3	C	'... there are more left-handed males than females.'
4	B	'... if a left-handed person is brain-damaged in the left hemisphere, the recovery of speech is quite often better ...'
5	A	3rd and 4th sentences of paragraph 3
6	C	'... discovered that the left-right asymmetry exists before birth.'
7	E	'He noted that this distinctive asymmetry in the human population is itself systematic.'

Questions 8–12

Question	Answer
8	15–20%
9	40%
10	6%
11	D
12	B

READING PASSAGE 2   *Migratory beekeeping*

Questions	Task	Skills tested
13–19	Completing a flow chart	• following a sequence of events • scanning/skimming for information • understanding gist and paraphrase
20–23	Labelling a diagram	• skimming for factual information • understanding description and relationships
24–27	Yes, No, Not Given	• skimming for factual information • understanding gist and paraphrase

Questions 13–19

Suggested approach

- Read the task rubric carefully. You have to complete the flow chart of the movements of a migratory beekeeper.
- Read through the flow chart to familiarise yourself with it.
- Scan the text and note the section that discusses the beekeepers' movements. In this case, the information is scattered throughout the text, so it is important to have a good idea of what you are looking for.
- Go back to the first box in the flow chart. Note that this box focuses on the start of migration.
- Re-skim the text until you come to this information. It is cued in the fourth paragraph: 'By early March ...'
- The flow chart will express the movements differently from the text. This is called 'paraphrasing'. The fourth paragraph is all about the beekeepers' preparations. So the answer to item 13 is 'prepare'.
- Go on to item 14. Remember that you will not use all the words in the box, and although some of the words in the box may seem to fit in the gaps, they have an incorrect meaning. Your summary must be an accurate reflection of what is stated in the passage.

Question	Answer	Location of answer in text
13	prepare	gist of paragraph 4
14	full	'These are not moved in the middle of the day because too many of the bees would end up homeless.'
15	smoke	'... bees can be pacified with a few puffs of smoke ...'
16	charge	'... the beekeeper will pay the farmer to allow his bees to feed ...'
17	machines	paraphrase of 'uncapper' and 'carousel'
18	combs	'... centrifugal force throws the honey out of the combs.'
19	split	'... a healthy double hive ... can be separated into two boxes.'

Questions 20–27

Question	Answer
20	(hexagonal) cells//comb
21	frames (of comb)
22	screen
23	brood chamber
24	NOT GIVEN
25	YES
26	YES
27	NO

READING PASSAGE 3   *Tourism*

Questions	Task	Skills tested
28–32	Paragraph headings	• detailed reading • identifying main ideas/themes/topics • understanding gist
33–37	Yes, No, Not Given	• skimming for detailed information • understanding paraphrase and gist • identifying attitude and opinion
38–41	Matching phrases	• skimming/scanning for detail • understanding paraphrase and gist • making inferences

Questions 28–37

Question	Answer
28	iii
29	v
30	iv
31	vii
32	viii
33	NO
34	YES
35	NOT GIVEN
36	YES
37	NOT GIVEN

Questions 38–41

Suggested approach

• Read the task rubric carefully. By choosing the correct phrase A–H, you will make summary points of the information given in the passage.
• It is obviously best to work from the questions as these are the start of each sentence.
• Read through item 38.
• Read through the list of phrases to familiarise yourself with them.
• Skim through the passage looking for key words that indicate that the information in question 38 is going to be discussed. For item 38, this occurs in paragraph B. In the middle of the paragraph you read: '... the

popular concept of tourism is that ...'. But to understand the entire point you will have to read the whole paragraph and take the gist. This is best summarised in the second sentence of the paragraph: 'It is one manifestation of how work and leisure are organised as separate and regulated spheres of social practice in 'modern' societies.' So the answer to question 38 is D.
• Go on to item 39 and repeat this procedure.

Question	Answer	Location of answer in text
38	D	'It is one manifestation of how work and leisure are organised as separate and regulated spheres ...'
39	B	'Such anticipation is constructed and sustained through a variety of non-tourist practices, such as film, TV ...'
40	F	'The viewing of these tourist sites often involves ... a much greater sensitivity to visual elements of landscape or townscape than is normally found in daily life.'
41	H	'... the mass tourist travels in guided groups and finds pleasure in inauthentic, contrived attractions ...'

PRACTICE TEST 3

LISTENING

Section 1

1 B
2 D
3 C
4 A
5 Richard Lee *(must have correct spelling of 'Lee' and capitals)*
6 30 Enmore Road *(must have correct spelling and capitals)*
7 Newport *(must have correct spelling and capital 'N')*
8 Architecture
9 LJX 058K
10 Ford
11 C
12 (on the) (front) window/windscreen

Section 2

13 November 1991
14 (historic) ships
15 green arrows
16 information desk
17 stairs to climb//lots of stairs
18 every hour
19 Captain Cook
20 the sea
21 Australian artists/painters
22 $70
23 souvenirs

Section 3

24 B
25 C
26 D
27 A
28 law has changed//law changes//changes in law
29 (powerful) computer programs
30 from home (computer)
31 hotels/hotel beds/rooms
32 hire cars

Section 4

33 displays//products//displays and products
34 (hidden) TV cameras
35 recorder//recording
36 'Spaceman'
37 position//shelf//spot//place
38 walk (straight/right) past // ignore//pass
39 at eye level//near customers' eyes
40 hotspots
41 special offers
42 chocolates

READING

READING PASSAGE 1   *Spoken corpus comes to life*

Questions	Task	Skills tested
1–6	Paragraph headings	• detailed reading • identifying main ideas/themes/topics • understanding gist
7–11	Labelling a diagram	• locating specific information • understanding a process • understanding paraphrase • distinguishing examples from main ideas
12	Global multiple choice	• identifying the overall intention of the writer

Questions 1–6

Question	Answer
1	vi
2	ii
3	x
4	viii
5	iv
6	ix

Questions 7–11

Suggested approach
- Read the task rubric carefully.
- Note that you must use a maximum of three words but that these do not have to be taken from the passage. Note also that you need to focus on particular paragraphs.
- Scan the diagram carefully and make sure you understand it. You have already read the passage once so you should realise that the diagram summarises most of the information in the passage.
- Look at item 7. This box describes an input into the Language Activator that is not part of the Spoken Corpus. Skim through the passage to find out what other kind of information is going into the Language Activator.
- The answer occurs at the beginning of paragraph C, although it is helpful to read

paragraph B too. An existing written corpus has been used.
- Repeat this procedure with the rest of the questions.

Question	Answer	Location of answer in text
7	existing	'This has been the basis – along with the company's existing written corpus ...'
8	(related) phrases	'... key words ... are followed by related phrases ...'
9	meanings// forms	gist of paragraph D
10	spoken// real//oral	'... written English works in a very different way to spoken English.'
11	noise// pauses// noises and pauses	'It also reveals the power of the pauses and noises we use to play for time, convey emotion, doubt and irony.'
12	B	

READING PASSAGE 2   *Moles happy as homes go underground*

Questions	Task	Skills tested
13–20	Paragraph headings	● detailed reading ● identifying main ideas/themes/topics ● understanding gist
21–26	Sentence completion	● skimming for factual information ● understanding description ● understanding paraphrase

Question 13–20

Question	Answer
13	xi
14	ix
15	viii
16	v
17	i
18	vii
19	iii
20	iv

Questions 21–26

Suggested approach

● Read the task rubric carefully. Note that you must use a maximum of three words for each answer, but that these do not have to be taken from the passage.
● You can take a straightforward approach to this set of questions as the items are not dependent upon each other.
● Read question 21 and note that you need to complete the sentence with the *reason why* developers prefer mass-produced housing.
● Skim through the text for a reference to *developers* and/or *mass-produced housing*.
● This information is located in paragraph F. Here you will read the sentence: 'In Europe, the obstacle has been conservative local authorities and *developers* who prefer to ensure quick sales with conventional *mass-produced housing*.'
● From this sentence you can understand that the reason why they prefer such housing is because it sells quickly.

● Read question 21 again remembering that you have to complete the sentence using a grammatically correct form of the answer. In this case, 'sell quickly' is the best answer.
● Repeat this procedure with items 22–26.

Question	Answer	Location of answer in text
21	sell (more) quickly	'In Europe the obstacle has been ... developers who prefer to ensure quick sales with conventional mass-produced housing.'
22	(South Limberg) planners	'... the Dutch development was greeted with undisguised relief by South Limburg planners ...'
23	(road/noise) embankments	'It was ... Hurkmans who hit on the idea of making use of noise embankments ...'
24	Olivetti employees	'... the Olivetti centre in Ivrea ... forms a house/hotel for Olivetti employees.'
25	adapt to	gist of paragraph H cued by 'Not everyone adapts so well ...'
26	his bakery business//a cool room	'Their home evolved when he dug a cool room for his bakery business in a hill he had created.'

READING PASSAGE 3 *A workaholic economy*

Questions	Task	Skills tested
27–32	Yes, No, Not Given	• skimming for detailed information • understanding gist and paraphrase • identifying attitude and opinion
33–34	Multiple choice	• skimming for information • identifying opinion • understanding paraphrase • distinguishing between main and supporting points
35–38	Selecting factors	• skimming for specific information • making inferences • understanding paraphrase

Questions 27–32

Suggested approach

- Read the task rubric carefully. Note that you have to make a judgement about the writer's views.
- Note, also, the difference between NO (which *contradicts* the writer's views) and NOT GIVEN (which means that the writer doesn't mention this at all).
- Read question 27. You have to decide whether the writer states that employees have fewer working hours today (compared with the past).
- Skim through the passage to see if you can come across this information or any contradictory information.
- The first paragraph states that working hours were reduced after the industrial revolution. However, in the second paragraph, the writer states that: '... working hours have increased noticeably since 1970 ...' and if you read on this fact is reiterated. So the statement (Q27) actually says the opposite of what the writer says. The answer to question 27 is therefore NO.
- Go on to item 28 and repeat this procedure.

Question	Answer	Location of answer in text
27	NO	'... working hours have increased noticeably since 1970 ...'
28	NOT GIVEN	
29	YES	'... real wages have stagnated since that year (1970).'
30	NO	'... the current economic recovery has gained a certain amount of notoriety for its "jobless" nature.'
31	YES	'She cites ... studies that show increased productivity for part-time workers ...'
32	NOT GIVEN	

Questions 33–38

Question	Answer	
33	C	
34	A	
35	B	*in*
36	D	*any*
37	F	*order*
38	G	

PRACTICE TEST 4

LISTENING

Section 1

1	C
2	A
3	B
4	D
5	D
6	Julia Perkins *(must be correct spelling with capital letters)*
7	15 Waratah Road *(must be correct spelling of Waratah with capital letter)*
8	Brisbane *(must have capital letter)*
9	to be advised//not connected//no phone// none *(blank not acceptable)*
10	first year Law *(must have all three words)*
11	C
12	D

Section 2

13	Hope Street *(must have capitals)*
14	evidence
15	passport
16	current/student (account)
17	chequebook
18	withdraw//draw (out)//take out
19	directly from//right out of
20	permission of/from bank
21	4.30 pm or/to 5 pm

Section 3

22	300 million
23	paper clips
24	magazine pages//pieces of paper//pages
25	three times
26	thicker
27	label
28	(a) dome
29	flange *(correct spelling)*
30	25%
31	scored opening

Section 4

32	a university lecture
33	Sports Studies (programme)
34	management
35	top athletes
36	makes winners//makes them/people win
37	market forces
38	(other) leisure activities
39	entertainment//to be entertained
40	exercise science
41	fitness testing//body measurements
42	cellular research//cellular change//body cells

READING

READING PASSAGE 1   *Glass*

Questions	Task	Skills tested
1–5	Paragraph headings	• reading for detail • identifying main ideas/themes/topics • understanding gist
6–8	Labelling a diagram	• following a description of a process
9–13	Classification	• skimming/scanning for specific information • understanding gist and paraphrase

Questions 1–5

Suggested approach
- Read the task rubric carefully. You have to decide which heading best fits each paragraph in the passage.
- Read paragraph A and look at the example.
- Skim through the list of paragraph headings to familiarise yourself with them.
- Read paragraph B and underline parts that are relevant to the main focus of the paragraph.
- Paragraph B begins 'On the horizon' suggesting that it is going to discuss a future use of glass. It goes on to discuss fibre optics and how they could be used in the future to improve optical instruments. Phrases such as 'could function hundreds of times faster' and 'the surge in fibre-optic use' all indicate that this paragraph is about 'Exciting innovations in fibre optics'. So **viii** is the heading for paragraph B.
- Go on to paragraph C.
- If you think there is more than one possible heading for a paragraph, re-read the paragraph and try to decide which heading is most appropriate.
- If you cannot decide, go on to the next paragraph – you can come back to any questions that you can't do, later.

Question	Answer	Focus of paragraphs
1	viii	The future of fibre optics and the excitement felt about this.
2	i	The increase in trade for glass artists.
3	ix	The impact of a machine for glass objects made in 1920.
4	iii	Reasons why glass is so easy to shape.
5	vi	The future with glass for designers of buildings and homes.

Questions 6–13

Question	Answer
6	molten glass//ribbon of glass// molten glass ribbon
7	belt of steel//steel belt//moving belt
8	(lightbulb) moulds
9	A
10	B
11	A
12	C
13	A

READING PASSAGE 2   *Why some women cross the finish line ahead of men*

Questions	Task	Skills tested
14–19	Identifying paragraphs	• skimming for detailed information • understanding paraphrase and summary
20–23	Matching	• skimming/scanning for speakers and information • understanding gist and paraphrase
24–27	Short-answer questions	• skimming for specific information • identifying question focus

Questions 14–23

Question	Answer
14	E
15	G
16	A
17	C
18	F
19	D
20	A
21	S
22	M
23	S

Questions 24–27

Suggested approach

- Read the task rubric carefully. Note that you must use a maximum of three words for each answer.
- You can take a straightforward approach to this set of questions.
- Read question 24. Note that it makes reference to 'the annual survey'.
- Skim through the text until it discusses an annual survey. This is in paragraph D.
- Look for a comment on changing numbers of female managers or directors. In the text, the survey is quoted as showing a 'doubling of the numbers'. Thus the *change* referred to in the question is the fact that the numbers have doubled.
- Read the question again to make sure you give a grammatically appropriate answer. In this case, the best answer would be 'it has

doubled' although 'double' alone would be acceptable because it is an understandable response to the question.
- Repeat this procedure with questions 25 to 27.

Question	Answer	Location of answer in text
24	(it has) double(d)// doubling	'This year the survey shows a doubling of the number of women serving as non-executive directors ...'
25	de-layering	'Sears said that this (de-layering) has halted progress for women ...'
26	demographic trends	'Demographic trends suggest that the number of women going into employment is steadily increasing.'
27	employers	'Until there is a belief among employers, until they value the difference, nothing will change.'

READING PASSAGE 3   *Population viability analysis*

Questions	Task	Skills tested
28–31	Yes, No, Not Given	• skimming for detailed information • understanding gist and paraphrase • identifying opinion
32–35	Matching (processes to paragraphs)	• detailed reading • identifying main and supporting points • understanding gist and paraphrase
36–38	Sentence completion	• skimming for information • understanding paraphrase
39	Global multiple choice	• understanding the overall theme of the passage

Questions 28–31

Question	Answer
28	YES
29	NO
30	NO
31	NOT GIVEN

Questions 32–35

Suggested approach
• Read the task rubric carefully. Note that these questions are based on Part B of the reading passage. You will have to decide which paragraphs in this part cover which processes.
• Note that there are two extra processes which are not described. The extra processes will be close to the correct answers but not correct. Read the text carefully so that you do not fall into any traps.
• Read through the list of processes to familiarise yourself with them.
• Read paragraph A carefully, noting any sections that relate to the processes described in **i – vi**.
• Paragraph A states that survival of a species is largely a 'matter of chance' and that not all animals produce young at the same rate. The meaning of this paragraph can therefore be glossed as 'the haphazard nature of reproduction' and **vi** is the correct answer to question 32.

• Repeat this procedure with questions 33–35.

Question	Answer	Focus of paragraph
32	vi	The fluctuation in reproduction rates.
33	iii	The problems of having a small or unequal number of one sex.
34	i	The effect on survival of an animal's ability to adapt to changes and therefore avoid extinction.
35	ii	The fluctuating environment in Australia, e.g. fire, flood and drought.

Questions 36–39

Question	Answer
36	will/may not survive//will/may/could become extinct
37	locality//distribution
38	logging takes place/occurs
39	B

GENERAL TRAINING

READING MODULE

PART 1

Questions	Task	Skills tested
1–4	Matching (pictures to text)	• detailed understanding of a section of text • understanding description of parts and their uses • identifying pictorial representation of text
5–8	Short-answer questions	• skimming for specific information • understanding description/characteristics • understanding paraphrase
9–14	Multiple choice	• skimming/scanning for specific information • understanding paraphrase • distinguishing between main and supporting points

Questions 1–8

Question	Answer
1	D
2	A
3	C
4	E
5	distilled (water)
6	the (type of) fabric
7	turn up/increase temperature
8	calcium deposits//furring up

Questions 9–14

Suggested approach

- Read the task rubric carefully. Only one option (A–D) is correct in each case.
- Read question 9 and the four options.
- Scan the headings in the text to see if any of them are about *seating* on the coach. The section entitled 'Seat Allocation' refers specifically to this.
- Skim through that section of the text and find out what you have to do if you want to sit at the front of the coach.
- This paragraph focuses entirely on the importance of booking early if you want a particular seat. So the answer to question 9 is C. Although all the other options are possible, only C is stated in the text.
- Repeat this procedure with questions 10–14.

Question	Answer	Location of answer in text
9	C	'Requests for particular seats can be made on most coach breaks when booking ...'
10	D	'... air or boat tickets may have to be retained and your driver or courier will then issue them to you at the relevant point.'
11	C	'If you require a special diet you must inform us at the time of booking ...'
12	A	'Other coach breaks have a limited number of rooms with private facilities ... the supplementary charge shown in the price panel will be added to your account.'
13	B	'The ... entertainment ... could be withdrawn if there is a lack of demand ...'
14	B	'... a small holdall can also be taken on board the coach.'

PART 2

Questions	Task	Skills tested
15–21	Matching (requirements to clubs)	• skimming/scanning for specific information • understanding paraphrase • making inferences
22–29	True, False, Not Given	• skimming/scanning for specific information • distinguishing between what is clearly stated and what is not stated. • understanding paraphrase and gist

Question 15–21

Question	Answer
15	E
16	D
17	A
18	E
19	A
20	B
21	F

Question	Answer	Location of answer in text
22	T	'long and short stays welcomed'
23	F	'You can join the Club ... for up to one year at a time.'
24	NG	
25	T	Gist of last part of Membership section.
26	T	'Thanks to the support of STA travel ... International Students House now provides the services of an International Students Adviser.'
27	NG	
28	NG	
29	F	'... the club will be offering reduced accommodation rates for students wishing to spend a few days in London over Christmas.'

Questions 22–29

Suggested approach

- Read the task rubric carefully. Note that you have to make a judgement about the list of statements.
- Note the difference between information that is false (i.e. the passage says the opposite) and information that is not given (i.e. not stated in the passage at all).
- Read question 22. This statement is about overnight accommodation.
- Scan the paragraph headings for a reference to accommodation. The first heading is 'Accommodation'.
- Skim through this section of the text to see if there is any information about how long you can stay at the club for. At the end of the section it states: 'long and short stays welcomed.' So the answer to question 22 is True.
- Repeat this procedure with questions 23–29.

PART 3

Questions	Task	Skills tested
30–36	Summary completion	• skimming for information • understanding paraphrase • rewording text
37–41	Flow chart completion	• skimming for specific information • following a process • summarising ideas

Questions 30–36

Suggested approach

- Read the task rubric carefully. You have to complete the summary by filling in the spaces with *words from the passage*. The words must fit in meaning and also be grammatically correct.
- Read the summary to familiarise yourself with it. It may be possible to find words without reading the original text, but if you do this you may pick words which are not in the text, in which case your answer will be *incorrect*. So you must look for a word within the passage which has the right meaning and which is the correct part of speech for the space.
- Read the first item in the summary.
- Look at the text and see if you can find the same information there. For item 30, the first sentence discusses the qualities of paper that make it different from other waste products. The text states that paper comes from a 'sustainable resource'. So 'sustainable' is a correct answer.
- Sometimes there are alternative answers that are correct in this type of question. For item 30, 'replaceable' is also a possible answer because it says a little further on in the text, 'trees are replaceable'.
- Note, however, that 'renewable' is not an acceptable answer because although it is a synonym and makes sense, it is not in the original text.

Question	Answer	Location of answer in text
30	sustainable//replaceable	'Paper ... comes from a sustainable resource ...'
31	biodegrad-able	'Paper is also biodegradable, so it does not pose as much threat to the environment when it is discarded.'
32	virgin fibre/pulp	'... the rest comes directly from virgin fibre ...'
33	governments//the government	'Governments have encouraged waste paper collection and sorting schemes ...'
34	advances	'... advances in the technology required to remove ink ...'
35	quality	'We need to accept a change in the quality of paper products'
36	contaminants	'... it also needs to be ... sorted from contaminants ...'

Questions 37–41

Question	Answer
37	offices
38	sorted
39	(re)pulped
40	de-ink//remove ink//make white
41	refined

ACADEMIC WRITING MODULE

Practice Test 3, Writing Task 1

You should spend about 20 minutes on this task.

> *The chart below shows the amount of money per week spent on fast foods in Britain. The graph shows the trends in consumption of fast-foods.*
>
> *Write a report for a university lecturer describing the information shown below.*

You should write at least 150 words.

Model answer 165 words

> The chart shows that high income earners consumed considerably more fast foods than the other income groups, spending more than twice as much on hamburgers (43 pence per person per week) than on fish and chips or pizza (both under 20 pence). Average income earners also favoured hamburgers, spending 33 pence per person per week, followed by fish and chips at 24 pence, then pizza at 11 pence. Low income earners appear to spend less than other income groups on fast foods, though fish and chips remains their most popular fast food, followed by hamburgers and then pizza.
>
> From the graph we can see that in 1970, fish and chips were twice as popular as burgers, pizza being at that time the least popular fast food. The consumption of hamburgers and pizza has risen steadily over the 20 year period to 1990 while the consumption of fish and chips has been in decline over that same period with a slight increase in popularity since 1985.

Practice Test 3, Writing Task 2

You should spend about 40 minutes on this task.

Present a written argument or case to an educated reader with no specialist knowledge of the following topic:

> *News editors decide what to broadcast on television and what to print in newspapers. What factors do you think influence these decisions? Do we become used to bad news? Would it be better if more good news was reported?*

You should write at least 250 words.

Use your own ideas, knowledge and experience and support your arguments with examples and relevant evidence.

Model answer: 300 words

It has often been said that 'Good news is bad news' because it does not sell newspapers. A radio station that once decided to present only good news soon found that it had gone out of business for lack of listeners. Bad news on the other hand is so common that in order to cope with it, we often simply ignore it. We have become immune to bad news and the newspapers and radio stations are aware of this.

While newspapers and TV stations may aim to report world events accurately, be they natural or human disasters, political events or the horrors of war, it is also true that their main objective is to sell newspapers and attract listeners and viewers to their stations. For this reason TV and radio stations attempt to reflect the flavour of their station by providing news broadcasts tailor-made to suit their listeners' preferences. Programmes specialising in pop music or TV soap operas focus more on local news, home issues and up-to-date traffic reports. The more serious stations and newspapers like to provide 'so called' objective news reports with editorial comment aimed at analysing the situation.

If it is true, then, that newspapers and TV stations are tailoring their news to their readers' and viewers' requirements, how can they possibly be reporting real world events in an honest and objective light? Many radio and TV stations do, in fact, report items of good news but they no longer call this news. They refer to these as human interest stories and package them in programmes specialising, for instance, in consumer affairs or local issues. Good news now comes to us in the form of documentaries: the fight against children's cancer or AIDS, or the latest developments in the fight to save the planet from environmental pollution.

GENERAL TRAINING WRITING MODULE

Writing Task 1

You should spend about 20 minutes on this task.

> *You have had a bank account for a few years. Recently you received a letter from the bank stating that your account is $240 overdrawn and that you will be charged $70 which will be taken directly from your account. You know that this information is incorrect.*
>
> *Write a letter to the bank. Explain what has happened and say what you would like them to do about it.*

You should write at least 150 words.

You do **NOT** need to write your own address.

Begin your letter as follows:

Model answer 186 words

Dear Sir,

I am writing in reply to a letter I received from you a few days ago. In your letter you state that I am $240 overdrawn and that you will be charging me $70.

I would like to point out that the reason I am overdrawn is because of a mistake made by your bank. If you look through your records you will see that I wrote several weeks ago explaining the situation. For the last twelve months, I have been paying $300 a month for a car I bought last summer. The monthly payments were taken directly from my bank account. However, two months ago I sold the car and I wrote to you instructing you to stop paying the monthly instalments. I received a letter from you acknowledging my request, but, for some reason, nothing was done about it. Another $300 instalment has been paid this month and this is the reason why I am overdrawn.

I would like you to contact the garage where I bought the car explaining your error. I would also like you to ask them to return the money.

Yours faithfully,

P Stoft

Writing Task 2

You should spend about 40 minutes on this task.

As part of a class assignment you have to write about the following topic:

> *We are becoming increasingly dependent on computers. They are used in businesses, hospitals, crime detection and even to fly planes. What things will they be used for in the future? Is this dependence on computers a good thing or should we be more suspicious of their benefits?*

You should write at least 250 words.

Model answer – 287 words

Computers are a relatively new invention. The first computers were built fifty years ago and it is only in the last thirty or so years that their influence has affected our everyday life. Personal computers were introduced as recently as the early eighties. In this short time they have made a tremendous impact on our lives. We are now so dependent on computers that it is hard to imagine what things would be like today without them. You have only got to go into a bank when their main computer is broken to appreciate the chaos that would occur if computers were suddenly removed world-wide.

In the future computers will be used to create bigger and even more sophisticated computers. The prospects for this are quite alarming. They will be so complex that no individual could hope to understand how they work. They will bring a lot of benefits but they will also increase the potential for unimaginable chaos. They will, for example, be able to fly planes and they will be able to co-ordinate the movements of several planes in the vicinity of an airport. Providing all the computers are working correctly nothing can go wrong. If one small program fails – disaster.

There is a certain inevitability that technology will progress and become increasingly complex. We should, however, ensure that we are still in a position where we are able to control technology. It will be all too easy to suddenly discover that technology is controlling us. By then it might be too late. I believe that it is very important to be suspicious of the benefits that computers will bring and to make sure that we never become totally dependent on a completely technological world.

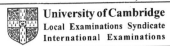

University of Cambridge
Local Examinations Syndicate
International Examinations

The British Council

IDP Education Australia
IELTS Australia

Centre number: **AA999**

Candidate name:

| 0 1 2 3 4 5 6 7 8 9 |
| 0 1 2 3 4 5 6 7 8 9 |
| 0 1 2 3 4 5 6 7 8 9 |
| 0 1 2 3 4 5 6 7 8 9 |

X

Please write your name above, then write your Candidate number
in the boxes on the right and shade the number in the grid.

Test date:

Day: 1 2 3 4 5 6 7 8 9 10 11 12 13 14 15 16 17 18 19 20 21 22 23 24 25 26 27 28 29 30 31

Month: 1 2 3 4 5 6 7 8 9 10 11 12   Last digit of the **Year:** 0 1 2 3 4 5 6 7 8 9

IELTS Listening Answer Sheet

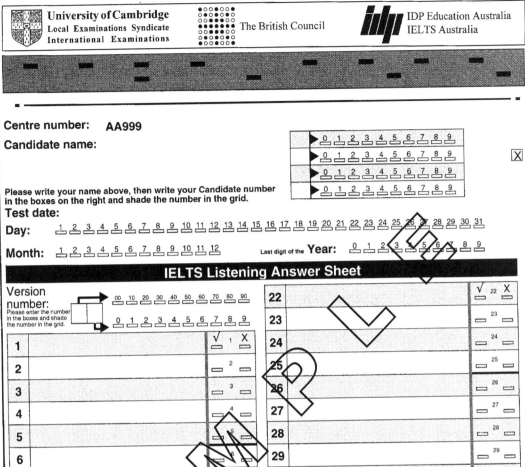

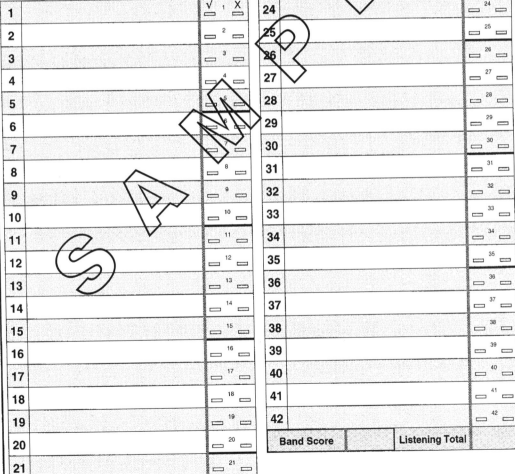

| Band Score | | Listening Total | |

IELTS L/R

© **UCLES/K&J** *You may photocopy this page.*

Module taken:

Academic ▭   General Training ▭

Version number:
Please enter the number
in the boxes and shade
the number in the grid.

00 10 20 30 40 50 60 70 80 90

0 1 2 3 4 5 6 7 8 9

#		✓ X
1		1
2		2
3		3
4		4
5		5
6		6
7		7
8		8
9		9
10		10
11		11
12		12
13		13
14		14
15		15
16		16
17		17
18		18
19		19
20		20
21		21
22		22
23		23
24		24
25		25
26		26
27		27
28		28
29		29
30		30

#		✓ X
31		31
32		32
33		33
34		34
35		35
36		36
37		37
38		38
39		39
40		40
41		41
42		42

Band Score		Reading Total

SAMPLE

Revised Speaking Module

From July 2001, there will be some revisions to the IELTS Speaking Module. The test maintains the one-to-one format, is rated on a scale of 1 to 9 as before and lasts for about 14 minutes. The main differences are in the overall format and nature of the tasks, which will now look like this.

Part 1 Introduction and interview 4 to 5 minutes	The examiner will introduce him/herself and check the identity of the candidate. The examiner will then ask the candidate a number of questions based on everyday topics, such as families, occupations, hobbies, hobbies, etc. using a set framework. Candidates should try to give a full answer to each question.	**Assessment** Throughout the test candidates will be assessed on their overall fluency, their vocabulary resource, and the range and accuracy of grammatical structures used. Pronunciation is very important and will also count towards the final score.
Part 2 Individual long turn 3 to 4 minutes	The candidate must speak for 1 to 2 minutes on a topic provided by the examiner. This will be written on a card. The candidate will have one minute to prepare what he/she is going to say. When the candidate has finished speaking, the examiner may ask one or two follow-up questions to round off this part of the test.	
Part 3 Two way discussion 4 to 5 minutes	The examiner will invite the candidate to discuss a number of issues linked broadly to the Part 2 topic. The candidate will be encouraged to develop language of a more abstract nature.	

Here are some Part 2 tasks. Each task is followed by an example of the type of questions which candidates will meet in Part 3 of the revised speaking test. However, these questions will not be presented in a written form in the real test but will be spoken by the examiner.

Test 1

Describe a photograph that you have taken yourself or seen in a book, which you particularly like.

You should say: what the picture shows
                   where you saw it
                   why you particularly like it

Do you like taking photographs/painting/drawing?
Do you prefer photographs or paintings?

Sample questions that the examiner could ask in Part 3

- *Explain the value of teaching art in primary and secondary schools.*
- *What is the role of traditional arts and crafts in your country?*
- *Are technology and the video camera changing our appreciation of photography?*

Test 2 Describe a character in a book you have read or a film you have seen.

You should say: why you chose this character
when you read the book/saw the film
how this character influenced you

Would you like to be like this character?
Do you know anyone who is like this character?

Sample questions that the examiner could ask in Part 3

• *What is the value of encouraging children to read stories or novels?*
• *How do you think authors create characters for their books? Where do these characters come from?*
• *Do you think film is the best medium for telling a story?*

Test 3 Describe your ideal home or place to live.

You should say: where it would be
how big it would be
what it would contain

Do you think you will live in this home one day?
Is this very different from your home today?

Sample questions that the examiner could ask in Part 3

• *What kind of homes do most people in your country live in?*
• *What are the advantages of living in an apartment?*
• *Is it the role of the state to provide subsidised housing for people on a low income?*

Test 4 Describe a wedding or celebration that you have attended which you enjoyed.

You should say: when the event took place
what happened
why you enjoyed it

Is this type of celebration popular in your country?
Have you been to a similar celebration since this one?

Sample questions that the examiner could ask in Part 3

• *How important is it to celebrate anniversaries or special days?*
• *What are the benefits of having national or public holidays?*
• *Is the concept of the 5-day working week and the 2-day weekend becoming out-of-date?*